unexpected
blessings

unexpected blessings

*The Joys & Possibilities
of Life in a
Special–Needs Family*

SANDRA PEOPLES

BETHANYHOUSE

a division of Baker Publishing Group
Minneapolis, Minnesota

Published by Bethany House Publishers
11400 Hampshire Avenue South
Bloomington, Minnesota 55438
www.bethanyhouse.com

Bethany House Publishers is a division of
Baker Publishing Group, Grand Rapids, Michigan

Printed in the United States of America

ISBN 978-0-7642-3166-7

Library of Congress Control Number: 2018940491

Scripture quotations are from The Holy Bible, English Standard Version® (ESV®), copyright © 2001 by Crossway, a publishing ministry of Good News Publishers. Used by permission. All rights reserved. ESV Text Edition: 2011

Cover design by Kathleen Lynch/Black Kat Design

Author represented by Karen Neumair of Credo Communications

18 19 20 21 22 23 24   7 6 5 4 3 2 1

To my mom and her friends,
who made the world a better place
for their kids and for mine:

Thresia Wood
Jessica Baldridge
Mary Sue Leu
Michelle Presley
Sharon Garrity

Contents

Introduction

Unexpected Circumstances, Unexpected Blessings

On November 16, 2010, our ship sailed into a tempest we had seen coming but hoped to avoid.

There had been signs. James didn't say as many words as most three-year-olds. We thought it was just because his big brother, David, never stopped talking. In an entire day, James said fewer than ten words, and not in sentences. Our good friend, an occupational therapist, pointed out that James didn't have motor skills expected for his age. He didn't play with toys appropriately. When he pushed a train along the track, he looked at the wheels, not the train itself. He didn't make eye contact, didn't respond when Daddy got home from work, and lost skills he had previously mastered (like forgetting the word *chartreuse*, which was his favorite color thanks to a *Blue's Clues* episode he watched over and over).

But it wasn't until we heard the psychologist say, "We believe your son has autism," that the full weight of the storm slammed into us, right there in a part-storage room, part-office space at our local elementary school. We sank deeper into the too-small chairs and looked at James as he tried to put a simple puzzle together with help from the occupational therapist assisting with the evaluation. He gave up quickly and tried to climb the shelves next to the window. A wave of thoughts hit me.

How different will things be now that James has a label, a diagnosis? How different will our family be? How will this affect our marriage? How will his big brother respond? What will their relationship be like? What will happen at church as he grows older but can't do what his peers can do? Everything seemed to change in that moment. They handed us a packet of information and gave us numbers to call for wait lists and more testing, then we took our son's hand—our autistic son's hand—and walked back out the doors of the school.

I accepted the inevitable and released my grip on the ship I had been sailing on for years. It was a ship of promise—I had promised God I would follow the rules and be a good girl, and I expected Him to promise me an easy life as a reward. I wanted sweet, smart boys, success in the ministry life we had devoted ourselves to, and no problems we couldn't solve with a quick library search or financial loan from my parents. These were the safety nets that had always caught me before.

My husband, Lee, refused to let go of his part of our battered ship. Built through his own hard work and determination, he thought anything could be accomplished with more effort. He would just add "Fix autism" to his to-do list and find a way to make it happen. His safety nets were his own efforts and resourcefulness.

Eventually, though, everything that had worked for us before failed, and we sank to the same spot.

Have you sunk too? Did you hear words from a teacher, a doctor, or a therapist that you keep repeating in your head—*cerebral palsy, Down syndrome, cognitive delays,* or even *diagnosis unknown?* Perhaps the piece of paper you received from the doctor has words like *deformity, motor skill delay, language delay, emotional disorder, hearing impairment,* or *seizure disorder.* You can't get past these labels and descriptions. You can't see around them. The path you thought you were walking took such a sharp detour that you can't see where it leads or even where to put your foot for the next step. It can feel overwhelming.

> My God, my God, why have you forsaken me? Why are you so far from saving me, from the words of my groaning? O my God, I cry by day, but you do not answer, and by night, but I find no rest.
>
> Psalm 22:1–2

> Save me, O God! For the waters have come up to my neck. . . . Let not the flood sweep over me, or the deep swallow me up, or the pit close its mouth over me.
>
> Psalm 69:1, 15

Are you in the tempest now? Overcome? You may find yourself in the same spot we were in as we sunk to the bottom— shipless. But please know, there's reason to hope.

> The floods have lifted up, O Lord, the floods have lifted up their voice; the floods lift up their roaring. Mightier than the thunders of many waters, mightier than the waves of the sea, the Lord on high is mighty!
>
> Psalm 93:3–4

> We went through fire and through water; yet you have brought us out to a place of abundance.
>
> Psalm 66:12

In the book of Acts, Paul was a prisoner on a ship heading to Rome when a tempest sent them way off course to the island of Malta. The battered crew and passengers certainly didn't know what to expect as they struggled to shore. Were more difficulties ahead? Instead, we're told they were met with "unusual kindness." Throughout *Unexpected Blessings*, we'll follow the example of Paul as we navigate our own way through the storms we are experiencing. We'll meet biblical characters and real-life friends of mine who found themselves in Plan B situations. The suffering was deep, the nights were long, the cycles of grief seemed to never end, but they all found hope to help them survive and eventually found a new purpose so they could thrive.

Charles Spurgeon, the great nineteenth-century preacher, said, "What if others suffer shipwreck, yet none that sail with Jesus have ever been stranded yet."[1] This was true for Job, Ruth, King David, Jonah, and Peter—they were never stranded. It's also true for me, my parents who have been caring for my sister with Down syndrome since her birth in 1977, and my friends Marie, Stephanie, and Greg. They took the same steps we are going to take in this book:

- evaluating the beliefs they held that weren't based on Scripture and therefore had to be replaced with true, biblical hope
- taking care of themselves through the storm
- getting to know a new group of people who could empathize
- making a positive difference in the place where they found themselves

I've been where you are today. Scared. Worried. Unsure what step to take next—unsure I could take the next step even if I knew what it was! But here we sit years later, my husband and I and other special-needs families, looking back on where

God has brought us. We accepted that not everything would go according to our own Plan A. We let go of what wasn't working for us anymore. We experienced the cycles of grief, and although they creep up occasionally, we have learned how to care for ourselves in tough times.

Lee and I met new people who understood our circumstances and could relate to our struggles. We even learned a new language—abbreviations like OT, PT, GF/CF, and ABA, plus all the insurance codes. But we no longer see our son's disability as something to fix, but as just part of who James is. We are still learning and growing, and I hope we never stop, but we are now to a point where we can give back to others on the same journey.

Soon after James's diagnosis, another mom with a son with autism encouraged me with this verse: "Those who sow in tears shall reap with shouts of joy!" (Psalm 126:5). Her son is my age, and she knew what we would face in the decades to come. That verse carries me through on the hardest days and makes the joyful days even more precious.

Our family has moved from a place of pain to having a purpose, and we can help you take that journey as well. The unexpected blessings you will experience will buoy you through the tough times, and with God's help, you will be able to look back with appreciation and joy.

one

Shipwreck

We must be willing to let go of the life we have planned, so as to have the life that is waiting for us.

E. M. Forster

In 2015, we packed up our lives and moved from rural Pennsylvania to suburban Texas. We left a church we loved serving for the previous eight years to start something new—planting a new church. Lee asked me how I felt about our new life, and I answered as I so often do when his big dreams change our plans, "Cautiously optimistic." It's kind of my motto. I'm not getting it tattooed anywhere soon, but I say it enough that Lee knows it will be my response to a fair share of questions. How do I feel about meeting James's new teacher? How do I feel about David auditioning for the next play? How do I feel about writing this book? How do I feel about going on a low carb diet for the month? *Cautiously optimistic.*

It's not that I'm a glass-half-empty kind of girl. It's just that I've been around the block enough times to know that things usually don't go as planned. And that makes me cautious. But I've also been pleasantly surprised how every Plan B situation has worked out for my good and spiritual growth, so that makes me optimistic.

Our vision for the new church was to be welcoming to people with disabilities from day one. We see special-needs families as an unreached people group, since so many don't attend church. They feel isolated and lonely, and they need the hope the gospel provides and the community a church offers. According to the last census data, almost 20 percent of families in the United States include someone with a disability, ranging from autism to Alzheimer's.[1] That's one in five families. And that's way too many who may feel like they have to stay home on a Sunday morning.

Before Lee and I even started our church, we worshiped and served with a nearby congregation that was going to help us get our ministry going. We got involved in the community with other churches in the area. To meet special-needs families, we did outreach events, including sensory-friendly movies and free family photo sessions with a photographer who was also a special education teacher. We met over two hundred special-needs families in the area through these events. Many told us, "Let us know when your church is open! We'd love to come!"

At the end of our first year in Texas, it was time to start our church. But after all those months of sharing our vision, only two families committed to coming with us (and one of those families knew they would be moving out of state after just a few months). Two more families we met from the community joined with us, but both drove over thirty minutes to our weekly Bible study and both have teenagers with disabilities, so it wasn't always easy for them to get out.

Through the second year we met weekly in our home for Bible study. We hired a babysitter for the younger kids, and the older kids and teens usually ate together and then joined us for Bible study time. Most weeks it was nine adults, four kids under ten years old (three with special needs), and nine older kids (four with special needs). We loved being together, and the other parents knew they could relax because their kids would be safe because of the precautions we had made to our home.

But after two years of funding from our supporting church, the local association of churches, and our state denomination, it was time for them to evaluate their investment in our new church. We needed to be more self-sustaining, but the families who met with us weren't able to give the amount we needed to make the budget work. My husband worked two jobs in addition to church planting, and I worked three part-time jobs from home. Still, without help from our funding sources, we couldn't continue to devote time and our own resources to keep the church going. In July 2017, we officially closed as Journey Church.

It's hard to see your dream die. Especially a church you hoped would be a source of hope, love, and community to people who need it all so desperately (like my family). Our Plan A didn't work out, but God wasn't finished with us.

No matter what diagnosis you've gotten, it likely wasn't your Plan A. My parents heard "Down syndrome" in the delivery room after they held my sister for the first time in 1977. It could have come months before if they had chosen to do an amniocentesis to test for chromosomal abnormalities, but it still would have been a surprise. I suspected James had autism (or at least sensory processing disorder and language delay) before he was diagnosed with autism, but it wasn't Plan A. And even if you read every word of the file on a child you are adopting, there will be surprises once he gets home and adjusts to life with your family.

When we switch from looking at the big picture to everyday challenges, we realize very few days go as planned. One phone call from the school nurse makes me leave an online meeting and hop in the car. One missing ingredient can change the dinner plan, a big deal when your child has food allergies or food aversions. A few drops of rain can bring the party inside, causing a meltdown for your daughter who had her heart set on swinging.

If it's true for a day, it's certainly true for the year, and it's especially true for a lifetime. None of us are living our Plan A scenario.

For list makers, menu planners, and routine keepers like me, that can be bad news. My automatic response isn't, "Oh well. It's going to be a great day/year/life anyway!" It's usually, "Nothing is going according to plan! I can't function without the plan!"

Writer Paul Virilio observed, "The invention of the ship was also the invention of the shipwreck."[2] We could say the invention of life was also the invention of a Plan B, at least from our human perspective. Adam and Eve thought their Plan A was to live in the garden of Eden forever. But sin entered through the choice they made, and so did their Plan B. But God came through with His Plan A—the redemption of the world through His Son Jesus Christ. He was fully God and fully man as He walked the earth two thousand years ago. He led a sinless life but took on the sins of the world, my sin and your sin. He alone could defeat death and restore our relationship with God, our creator. When we place our faith in Him and what He accomplished for us, we are adopted into God's family and become coheirs with Christ. The Holy Spirit abides in us and guides our thoughts, actions, and feelings. As sons and daughters of God, we can take each step He asks of us on this journey.

From Adam and Eve to now, each person has lived out his or her own Plan B. We see this throughout Scripture, including the accounts of Job, Ruth, Jonah, and Peter.

Job—Steadfast Hope

One of the most drastic Plan B lives we see in the Bible is Job's. A righteous man, who like me probably believed he had earned an easy life since he was so good at following the rules, found himself sitting in a pile of rubble and dust, both figuratively and literally. He lost his children, his livestock, his servants, and his health. Yet, we're told he worshiped even after receiving so much devastating news (see Job 1:20). And after his wife told him to curse God and die, Job responded, "Shall we receive good from God, and shall we not receive evil?" (2:10).

The rest of the long book of Job records conversations between Job and his friends and Job and God. Job mourned the life he'd been given: "I will speak in the anguish of my spirit; I will complain in the bitterness of my soul. . . . I loathe my life; I would not live forever" (7:11, 16).

What did he want most of all? Someone to bridge the gap between himself and God: "There is no arbiter between us, who might lay his hand on us both" (9:33). He wanted to enter God's presence and hear from Him: "Oh, that I knew where I might find him, that I might come even to his seat!" (23:3). But even if Job had to live this life of suffering until he died, he still had hope. Hope that there was a purpose to his Plan B life: "I know that you can do all things, and that no purpose of yours can be thwarted" (42:2).

Ruth—Follow God's Leading

Ruth experienced what we can assume was a good life early on. She lived in her homeland with her husband and had a close relationship with his family who had come to Moab from Bethlehem before the head of the family, Elimelech, passed away. After ten years of marriage, her husband and her brother-in-law died, leaving Ruth with her mother-in-law Naomi and the widow of her brother-in-law, Orpah. This was certainly not Plan A for this young woman who didn't have any children of her own.

But she (being braver and more optimistic than I am) went all in on Plan B, moving back to Bethlehem with Naomi, "For where you go I will go, and where you lodge I will lodge. Your people shall be my people, and your God my God" (Ruth 1:16). How scared she must have been on that journey to an unknown place. Especially when Naomi encouraged her to turn back as Orpah decided to do. But Ruth had learned enough about the true God from her husband and his family to know that where His people were was a safe place for her as well. John Piper reflects on the life of Ruth, "When you think [God] is farthest from you, or has even turned against you, the truth is that as you cling to him, he is laying foundation stones of greater happiness in your life."[3]

Ruth's story took some twists and turns once they were back in Naomi's homeland, but God guided Ruth's decisions, and she married Boaz and gave birth to Obed, who is the father of Jesse, the father of David, and in the lineage of Christ Himself. The people of Bethlehem, who had heard Naomi (which meant *pleasant*) change her name to Mara (meaning *bitter*), rejoiced with her, saying, "Your daughter-in-law who loves you, who is more to you than seven sons, has given birth to him" (4:15). As the *Women's Evangelical Commentary* points out, this is "an amazing statement in a culture in which sons were highly esteemed. This supreme compliment surely refers not only to Ruth's character (3:11) but also to her unusual commitment to care unselfishly for her aged, and even embittered, mother-in-law."[4] Ruth felt safety and security even in her Plan B life, and so can you as you follow God's leading and rest in His presence.

Jonah—God Knows Best

Jonah is one of my favorite Plan B stories because God gave him a clear Plan A and he came up with his own Plan B! God had to bring Jonah back to His purpose for him.

The book of Jonah gets right into the action with God saying to Jonah, "Arise, go to Nineveh, that great city, and call out against it, for their evil has come up before me" (Jonah 1:2), but Jonah went a different direction: "Jonah rose to flee to Tarshish from the presence of the Lord" (v. 3).

Jonah boarded a ship and, like us, encountered a storm. Even the ship's crewmen who did not know Jonah's God realized God was indeed real and trying to get Jonah's attention. "The men were exceedingly afraid and said to him, 'What is this that you have done!' For the men knew that he was fleeing from the presence of the Lord, because he had told them" (v. 10). God used the fierce storm to convince the crew to throw Jonah overboard as Jonah asked them to do, "So they picked up Jonah and hurled him into the sea, and the sea ceased from its raging. Then the men feared the Lord exceedingly, and they offered a sacrifice to the Lord and made vows" (vv. 15–16).

Most preschool age Sunday school classes can tell you what happened next—a great big fish swallowed Jonah, and he lived in the belly of the fish for three days and nights. Thankfully, you and I have never been in the belly of a fish. But we have felt lost, in the dark, and separated from the life we knew. You may even relate to Jonah's description: "For you cast me into the deep, into the heart of the seas, and the flood surrounded me; all your waves and your billows passed over me" (2:3). But Jonah knew this suffering served a purpose. That God had a plan for him.

Jonah prayed to God, and God answered his prayers by having the fish deposit Jonah onto the shore. Jonah fulfilled the calling God had given him when we first met Jonah: "Jonah began to go into the city, going a day's journey. And he called out, 'Yet forty days, and Nineveh shall be overthrown!' And the people of Nineveh believed God. They called for a fast and put on sackcloth, from the greatest of them to the least of them" (3:4–5). After they repented, "God saw what they did, how they turned from their evil way, [and he] relented of the disaster that he had said he would do to them, and he did not do it" (3:10).

It would be a good story if it ended there, but it doesn't. Jonah was mad at God for having compassion on such sinful people. "Jonah went out of the city and sat to the east of the city and made a booth for himself there. He sat under it in the shade, till he should see what would become of the city" (4:5). God grew up a plant to shade Jonah but caused it to die the next day. When Jonah was sad about the loss of the plant, God reminded him the lives of the people of Nineveh were even more important than the plant. God's care for Nineveh is clear in this story, but so is His care for Jonah. God's love is big and wide, and also personal and specific. We see both on our Plan B journey.

Peter—It Starts with a Decision

Peter's Plan B story is a dream for all the dreamers. You're at work one day, doing what you always do, and then someone makes an offer you can't refuse. When Peter and his brother Andrew heard Jesus say, "Follow me, and I will make you fishers of men," Matthew writes, "Immediately they left their nets and followed him" (Matthew 4:19–20). One minute Plan A, the next minute Plan B. I'm sure Peter was excited, but he also had to be scared. Where would they sleep that night? What would they have for dinner? Peter strikes me as enough of an optimist to assume it was all going to work out fine, even without a plan. They were familiar with the ministry of John the Baptist and had heard of this new teacher from Nazareth. Peter felt God's call on his life, and he followed in obedience.

It reminds me of the moment my parents got my sister's diagnosis of Down syndrome. There were no hints, no clues before she was born that anything would be different from all the other babies born two days after Christmas in 1977. But not only was she born with Down syndrome, she was also born with an intestinal blockage. Her body would not be able to process any nourishment. Syble was put on a helicopter to Oklahoma City for emergency surgery, and my parents got in an ambulance to follow as quickly as they could. This was certainly not Plan A for my mom and dad, who were just twenty-six at the time and having their first child.

At the hospital in Oklahoma City, a young doctor took my dad into a janitor's closet and said to him, "Look, your daughter has two issues. One will kill her. One will affect her life and yours forever. If you don't want us to fix the intestinal blockage and let her die, we would understand that choice." But like Peter, my dad was enough of an optimist to know it would all work out okay. And he knew my sister was part of God's purpose for his life. Other hard decisions would come (What therapies does she need? What can we do now to help her be independent in the future? When should we have more children? Will they also have Down syndrome?), but the first decision in that janitor's closet was an easy one.

Peter's first decision to leave the fishing boat and follow Jesus was an easy one too. A sharp turn from Plan A to Plan B. But that didn't make for an easy road. Peter certainly had highs and lows in the three years he walked with Christ, seeing Him perform miracles, forgive sins, command the weather, and even rise from the dead. Even when Peter betrayed his friend and teacher, Jesus never gave up on him. He kept Peter moving forward to fulfill the purpose He had for his life.

Everyone Lives a Plan B Life

When we receive a diagnosis, we can feel like the only ones who have ever been so devastated, so rocked to our core. But we see from the lives of Job, Ruth, Jonah, and Peter that no one is truly living their Plan A life. We all go through a shipwreck of sorts and have to survive the aftermath. You may feel alone and adrift, but God never takes His eyes off you. There's a short phrase in the middle of one of the best-known psalms that brings me comfort: "you are with me" (Psalm 23:4). He is with you.

Even more than you can imagine, He is grieved by the effects of sin we have to deal with on earth. It wasn't part of His original plan. A scene from *The Magician's Nephew* by C. S. Lewis illustrates this well:

> "But please, please—won't you—can't you give me something that will cure Mother?"
>
> Up till then he had been looking at the Lion's great feet and the huge claws on them; now, in his despair, he looked up at its face. What he saw surprised him as much as anything in his whole life. For the tawny face was bent down near his own and (wonder of wonders) great shining tears stood in the Lion's eyes. They were such big, bright tears compared with Digory's own that for a moment he felt as if the Lion must really be sorrier about his mother than he was himself.
>
> "My son, my son," said Aslan. "I know. Grief is great."[5]

Once we accept that Plan B is the new Plan A, we can move forward to heal and discover God's new purpose for our lives. The process isn't easy, but it's worth it. When you accept your

Plan B, you can be assured God will be there every step of the way with His peace, provision, presence, and power.

Even through all of his struggles, Job held on to the peace that surpasses all understanding: "For I know that my Redeemer lives, and at the last he will stand upon the earth" (Job 19:25). At the end of the book of Job, God provided him with a family and wealth again. But it was the peace of seeing God's faithfulness that he carried with him until his death: "And after this Job lived 140 years, and saw his sons, and his sons' sons, four generations. And Job died, an old man, and full of days" (42:16–17). Do you feel that peace? Some days you have to fight for it—you fall asleep praying God would surround you with His peace. But having a relationship with the Prince of Peace means His peace is yours, and you can learn to receive and rest in it.

God's provision for Ruth and Naomi was clear every step of their journey. Although they started out desperate and poor, when they arrived back in Bethlehem, God led Ruth to glean in Boaz's field. Boaz noticed her and asked his men to make sure Ruth got what she needed. After following the advice of Naomi, Boaz became Ruth's kinsman redeemer, a provision God had ordained generations before to protect vulnerable widows. Each time Ruth had a decision to make, God's provision was apparent. Have you seen it in your life? Maybe a friend shared an article that led you to find a solution for your family. Or a doctor knew exactly what test to order next. We find God's provision everywhere when we take time to look and give thanks.

God's presence was with Jonah on the ship, in the belly of the great fish, as he preached a message of repentance in Nineveh, and when he pouted on the hillside. His presence was clear when He provided a vine to shade Jonah and teach him a lesson about what Jonah should truly value. God showed His care for the great city of Nineveh and for Jonah as he sat alone. He was omnipresent from ocean depths to hillsides. Do you think you've moved so far away from God that He may not be able to find you? That your confusion, anger, or bad decisions hide you from Him? That could never be true. His love is deep and wide and expands to reach you wherever you find yourself.

Peter had a front-row seat to see God's power on display through the life of His Son. He saw Jesus's power over nature when He walked on water, over demons as He cast them out of the people they tormented, over disease as He healed the woman subject to bleeding and many others, over death as He raised Lazarus, and over sin as He defeated it with His death and resurrection. Can you feel it when you are woken up yet again at three in the morning and you are still able to care for your child with love? Do you see it when your typical daughter defends her sister against teasing at school? And when you can look at a family member who hurt you with his words and actions and offer forgiveness, you know that is God's power working in and through you.

Are you ready to see more of God's peace, provision, presence, and power for yourself? It's all there—on your Plan B path.

To Discuss or Journal

1. Do you consider yourself an optimist, pessimist, or realist? What experiences in your life led you to the personality type you tend to be?
2. Have you made a profession of faith in Christ? If so, share how that has made a difference in how you see your current circumstances. If not, think and pray about making that decision today. Talk to a friend or pastor about the steps to take next.

3. How do you feel today about your life taking this Plan B turn?

4. Which Plan B story do you relate to most—Job, Ruth, Jonah, or Peter? What stands out to you about your similar journeys?

5. God's peace, provision, presence, and power are all available to you today. Which one do you need to be reminded of? Pray for God to display it in your life.

two

Letting Go

When our dream becomes a demand, it takes center place where only God should be.

Paul E. Miller, *A Loving Life*

Our friends had just gotten back from Hawaii and were sharing stories and pictures from their trip.

"The funniest thing we noticed on our flight and at the hotel where we stayed was the number of men who kept playing with their wedding rings. They would spin or rub or just touch them so often we made a game out of spotting them. After striking up a few conversations, we realized they were honeymooners! New husbands who weren't used to wearing their wedding rings yet."

Their wedding rings and their inability to stop playing with them were signs of change in their lives. Changes they were still adjusting to.

For the rest of us, signs of change may include moving boxes, stretch marks, and piles of too-small clothes. But other signs of change can't be seen by others—we can only feel them. Some changes are so big we are never the same again. Our foundations have shifted, our ships are going down, and we have to change and adapt or be left behind.

On Paul's ship, things were going well. Until they weren't. "Now when the south wind blew gently, supposing that they had obtained their purpose, they weighed anchor and sailed along Crete, close to the shore. But soon a tempestuous wind, called the northeaster, struck down from the land" (Acts 27:13–14). These experienced sailors knew what to do to protect themselves, the cargo, and the ship. But would it be enough? Or would they have to let go?

Leading up to James's Diagnosis

After being completely honest with our pediatrician at James's three-year well visit and her encouraging me to find out more about his delays, I had finally called the school to schedule an evaluation for James, but it would be a couple of weeks before they could see us. I was frustrated at myself for waiting so long to call, and then it would take even longer. While we waited, I did what I always do—I read books.

I read some pages through tears and some with relief. I found James in each chapter of these books. Did you know most autistic children don't point? I didn't know that. James didn't point. Walking on tiptoes? Also common for children with autism. As scared as I was of the autism diagnosis, I was relieved to find a label for all he did that was different. A label meant my child was not the only child who was like this. It meant someone else would have answers. Above all, it meant we weren't the only ones. If he did have autism, we could get help—for him and for us.

The books on autism were answering my questions about characteristics and treatment options, but I was struggling with deeper questions as well. I was angry at God. I didn't believe I deserved to have a special-needs child. God owed me better. I wrestled with this issue for weeks. Why was I being punished? Why wasn't I getting what I felt I deserved? God continued to draw me to Himself and to His Word.

I found a kindred spirit in Paul, who wrote, "I myself have reason for confidence in the flesh also. If anyone else thinks he has reason for confidence in the flesh, I have more: circumcised on the eighth day, of the people of Israel, of the tribe of Benjamin, a Hebrew of Hebrews; as to the law, a Pharisee; as to zeal, a persecutor of the church; as to righteousness under the law, blameless" (Philippians 3:4–6). Look at all the reasons he had to boast, feel proud, and even feel entitled! How did Paul keep from sinning after looking at his impressive resume? He wrote,

> But whatever gain I had, I counted as loss for the sake of Christ. Indeed, I count everything as loss because of the surpassing worth of knowing Christ Jesus my Lord. For his sake I have suffered the loss of all things and count them as rubbish, in order that I may gain Christ and be found in him, not having a righteousness of my own that comes from the law, but that which comes through faith in Christ, the righteousness from God that depends on faith—that I may know him and the power of his resurrection, and may share his sufferings, becoming like him in his death, that by any means possible I may attain the resurrection from the dead.
>
> Philippians 3:7–11

Like Paul, I could think of all the things I've done right. All the rules I've followed. All the traditions I've kept. I became a Christian at six years old and was baptized. I attended church as often as possible when growing up. I was a leader in my youth group and then in my college group. I've taken mission trips. I went to a Christian university and then to seminary. I've led Bible studies, taught Sunday school classes, and spoken at women's events. I married a pastor. I read the Bible to my boys. I pray with them and over them. I listen to Christian music. We sacrifice time, money, and the "pleasures of the world" for ministry and for God. But listing everything I think I've done right doesn't make me more like Christ; it makes me more like the Pharisees He spoke out against.

Paul had been a Pharisee, but meeting Christ had humbled him. He combated the sins of pride and entitlement with the power of the cross. Like Paul's, my list of accomplishments pales in comparison to the life of Christ. When I compare all my good deeds to His death on the cross, I am reminded of what a sinner I am. I'm also reminded of His grace and love and that I don't have to do every good work to earn His love, but I am able to do good works because of His love.

Paul writes in Ephesians, "For by grace you have been saved through faith. And this is not your own doing; it is the gift of God, not a result of works, so that no one may boast. For we are his workmanship, created in Christ Jesus for good works, which God prepared beforehand, that we should walk in them" (2:8–10). Grace and faith are gifts from God I didn't have to earn. I just accept them and live them out by taking the steps He has laid out for me, including the opportunities I have to show His love to others, the good works He prepared beforehand.

Dangerous Beliefs

As I worked through my sins of pride and entitlement, I also had to work through lots of questions. Was I being punished? Was there a lesson I was supposed to learn? If I was supposed to learn a lesson, why couldn't there be another way? Why did my son have to suffer so I could learn a lesson?

I realized beliefs from what some refer to as the prosperity gospel had crept into my faith foundation. Any time a word gets added to *gospel*, the results take us away from its true message. And the prosperity gospel is one of the worst offenders. I don't want to breeze past this. I truly believe this is the most dangerous belief system special-needs parents are influenced by because it puts a burden on us we don't need to carry. You can be crushed by its power. And it isn't about a specific pastor or church you may associate with the phrase. Every one of us deals with this on some level, and we need to dig it out by the root and find freedom from it.

Here are five signs that, like me, you may be more influenced by a subverted gospel than you realize:

1. You believe you and your family members shouldn't suffer. Is there a single person in the Bible who didn't suffer? Jesus Himself is referred to as the Suffering Servant. If you believe you shouldn't suffer based on your own actions, you are implying Jesus's actions caused Him to deserve His horrific suffering. That's not just dangerous, that's heretical.

2. You believe those who don't have the same advantages you do don't deserve them. Do you look at others and assume they don't have what you have because they did something wrong? Or a previous generation in their family did something wrong?

3. You have an *us vs. them* mentality. Do you look around and see scarcity? Like there's never enough money, time, jobs, or opportunities, and if you don't grab what's yours, someone else will? That's not God's economy. He lavishes love and grace on all His children. He doesn't run out for those at the end of the line.

4. You empower self instead of deny self. Our society puts a lot of focus on the self. Just think of all the words that start with it: self-esteem, self-empowerment, self-fulfillment. To be happy is seen as the highest goal. But we are not of this world. Our goal is higher—to have the mind of Christ (see 1 Corinthians 2:16). And He set the example of service and love, even to those we could consider enemies. The gospel you believe should compel you to put others' needs before your own.

5. You feel like you "do" and therefore you "deserve." I know this lie well. Those of us who are hard workers and rule followers wish it were true. And maybe it was in your house growing up—you got good grades and were rewarded, but your brother got bad grades and was punished. You both got what you deserved. But grace gives you more than you deserve. As we saw in the life of Paul, our good works don't compare to the works of Christ on our behalf.

I can share these signs with you because at times I've seen them in my own life. They creep in and whisper their lies, and they seem to make sense, especially in our American or Western context. But if the message we believe isn't true for everyone in the world, from the penthouses in Qatar to the crowded streets of Mozambique, then the message isn't true. It doesn't depend on what you have or don't have, what you do or don't do. The gospel is good news for all people.

The book of James says "Every good gift and every perfect gift is from above, coming down from the Father of lights, with whom there is no variation or shadow due to change" (1:17). It's easy to see what we would consider as good and perfect gifts coming from God: good health, happy and obedient kids, pretty weather, and extra quality time with our spouses. These are all good gifts. But we must also consider the hard things good and perfect gifts. You can look back on your life and see times when that was true, right? A cancer diagnosis is bad, but it can bring a feuding family together to support the person going through chemo. Losing a job is bad, but it can help you assess your priorities and guide you to making a different decision about your future.

When I change my perspective and see everything as coming from God, the problems don't feel as overwhelming. I can pray, "God, thank you for trusting me with this responsibility. I want to glorify You in everything, including this challenge. I need Your help to not grow resentful, but to see this from Your perspective, as a good and perfect gift."

Nancy Guthrie writes, "What allows us as God's children to endure it is that while it's painful, we're confident it's purposeful. Never punitive. Never random. Never too harsh. Always out of love. What's the purpose? God's desire is that 'afterward there will be a peaceful harvest of right living for those who are trained in this way' (Hebrews 12:11). God is at work cutting away the dead places and destructive patterns in our lives so we can flourish and grow."[1]

Multiple times every day I had to repeat to myself, "God loves me. God loves James." Again and again I said it. I said it until I believed it. False promises of a struggle-free life are lies and can't stand up against the truth of God's grace and love. His gifts are actually bigger than what we deserve, earn, or work so hard for. We just have to shift our perspective to see these gifts correctly.

Getting to Know God Better

Just a few months ago I learned something about my husband I didn't know before—he had never cleaned a fish. I grew up in

Oklahoma, the tomboy daughter of a fishing dad, so I could bait a hook, cast a line, and clean a fish to get it ready to fry up. But Lee didn't have those same experiences. When my dad took our older son out to fish on his boat and then showed him how to clean his catch, Lee looked on with interest. No matter how well we think we know someone, there's always more to learn. And sometimes we have to unlearn what we thought we knew to make room for the truth.

Many people relate to God in the ways they learned to relate to their fathers. If Dad was authoritarian and punitive, God is too. If Dad was distant and standoffish, God is too. If Dad withheld love and affection until your actions or behaviors fit what he wanted from you, God will too. Often these ideas are so deeply ingrained, we don't know we think them until we're in a situation when we expect the worst out of God.

The blessings of this storm and of our ship going down are that we get to know God in new and better ways. Like being in the calm eye of a hurricane with wind and rain all around us but not touching us, we suddenly see God is there and He is for us. He is in the storm and in the calm. We no longer cling to our ideas of Him—we can only cling to Him. Like Mary Magdalene after the resurrection, we want to hold on to our idea of Him, but He gently points us to something better:

> But Mary stood weeping outside the tomb, and as she wept she stooped to look into the tomb. And she saw two angels in white, sitting where the body of Jesus had lain, one at the head and one at the feet. They said to her, "Woman, why are you weeping?" She said to them, "They have taken away my Lord, and I do not know where they have laid him." Having said this, she turned around and saw Jesus standing, but she did not know that it was Jesus. Jesus said to her, "Woman, why are you weeping? Whom are you seeking?" Supposing him to be the gardener, she said to him, "Sir, if you have carried him away, tell me where

you have laid him, and I will take him away." Jesus said to her, "Mary." She turned and said to him in Aramaic, "Rabboni!" (which means Teacher). Jesus said to her, "Do not cling to me, for I have not yet ascended to the Father; but go to my brothers and say to them, 'I am ascending to my Father and your Father, to my God and your God.'" Mary Magdalene went and announced to the disciples, "I have seen the Lord"—and that he had said these things to her.

John 20:11–18

Mary wanted to hold on to the teacher she knew so well, but she had to let go. Jesus told her His work wasn't done yet, the story wasn't complete. He would go to His Father and the Holy Spirit would indwell us. But we're scared of what we don't know. We'd rather hold on to what's comfortable, even if it isn't working. I can look at my shoe collection and see that! Sure this pair of heels pinches, but when will I have time and money to shop for a new pair? I'll just limp around church one more morning.

Elijah

Mary of Magdalene isn't the only one who had her perspective changed after a major life event. One of my husband's favorite Bible stories is what he calls "The Showdown at Mount Carmel" in 1 Kings 18. (He grew up watching wrestling, like WWE wrestling, and especially loved the showmanship on display. This story has trash talk and showmanship aplenty!) The scene is set starting in verse 17:

When Ahab saw Elijah, Ahab said to him, "Is it you, you troubler of Israel?" And he answered, "I have not troubled Israel, but you have, and your father's house, because you have abandoned the commandments of the Lord and followed the Baals. Now therefore send and gather all Israel to me at Mount Carmel, and the 450 prophets of Baal and the 400 prophets of Asherah, who eat at Jezebel's table."

Elijah and the prophets of Baal had their showdown. The challenge was for fire to come down and burn up each sacrifice. The prophets of Baal went first:

> And they took the bull that was given them, and they prepared it and called upon the name of Baal from morning until noon, saying, "O Baal, answer us!" But there was no voice, and no one answered. And they limped around the altar that they had made. And at noon Elijah mocked them, saying, "Cry aloud, for he is a god. Either he is musing, or he is relieving himself, or he is on a journey, or perhaps he is asleep and must be awakened."
>
> vv. 26–27

Elijah built an altar to the Lord and made it even harder for anyone to deny who was the most powerful—he soaked the offering and wood three times. He prayed and "then the fire of the Lord fell and consumed the burnt offering and the wood and the stones and the dust, and licked up the water that was in the trench. And when all the people saw it, they fell on their faces and said, 'The Lord, he is God; the Lord, he is God'" (vv. 38–39).

I imagine Elijah was feeling pretty good after this. His actions had led to God showing up in a powerful way and many of his enemies were humiliated and destroyed. What he thought would happen did happen. Verse 46 says, "The hand of the Lord was on Elijah." I feel like up to the point of James's diagnosis that could have been said of my life. I could easily look back and see how God was guiding me and providing for me. Even when I hit problems, they were easily solved. But like in my life, Elijah experienced a challenge he felt was too much to ask of him, and he began to doubt God's plan.

After the showdown, Ahab reported to Jezebel all that had happened, and she sent word to Elijah that she would kill him within twenty-four hours. Elijah fled into the wilderness, sat under a tree after a day's journey, and asked God to take his life (see 19:4). Instead he slept and God sent an angel with food and water for Elijah. He then journeyed to Horeb, the mount of God, and found shelter in a cave (see vv. 8–9).

God spoke to Elijah and asked, "What are you doing here?" God listens to our words and our groanings. He even hears words we're unable to speak when we aren't sure what to pray. Romans 8:26 says, "Likewise the Spirit helps us in our weakness. For we do not know what to pray for as we ought, but the Spirit Himself intercedes for us with groanings too deep for words." Elijah answered God's question by reminding God of all Elijah had done for Him and insisting he did not deserve to be treated this way: "I, even I only, am left, and they seek my life, to take it away" (1 Kings 19:10). God replied:

> "Go out and stand on the mount before the Lord." And behold, the Lord passed by, and a great and strong wind tore the mountains and broke in pieces the rocks before the Lord, but the Lord was not in the wind. And after the wind an earthquake, but the Lord was not in the earthquake. And after the earthquake a fire, but the Lord was not in the fire. And after the fire the sound of a low whisper.
>
> vv. 11–12

I love how God shows up when we are at our worst. He is gentle and kind. There may be wind, earthquakes, and fire around us, but you hear a song or a sermon that begins to heal your heart. Your Scripture reading leads you to passages that remind you of His love and grace. The Holy Spirit prompts a friend to text or call at exactly the right time. Or God simply yet powerfully blesses you with a sense of peace that surpasses all understanding—a whisper.

All God told Elijah that would happen after this encounter happened. But Elijah was a new man. The foundation he had laid for himself—the idea that God was wind, earthquake, and fire—dissolved into a power that didn't show off. God's power moved with the power of a whisper, and His will was still accomplished. Elijah learned to look for God in new places and see His hand doing new things. We can do that in our own lives as well.

When Hope Was Abandoned, God Showed Up

When we catch up with Paul and the ship's crew at sea in the storm, we see his encouragement to the others:

> Since we were violently storm-tossed, they began the next day to jettison the cargo. And on the third day they threw the ship's tackle overboard with their own hands. When neither sun nor stars appeared for many days, and no small tempest lay on us, all hope of our being saved was at last abandoned.
>
> Since they had been without food for a long time, Paul stood up among them and said, "Men, you should have listened to me and not have set sail from Crete and incurred this injury and loss. Yet now I urge you to take heart, for there will be no loss of life among you, but only of the ship."
>
> Acts 27:18–22

They weren't going to die, but they would lose the ship. Can you imagine the fear? If you've seen movies about the Titanic sinking, I'm sure you can. The ship is all you have when you're in the middle of the sea. It's stay on the ship or die. But the truth is it's not the ship or any man-made object that saves us.

Some trust in chariots and some in horses,
    but we trust in the name of the Lord our God.
Psalm 20:7

For not in my bow do I trust,
    nor can my sword save me.
Psalm 44:6

The king is not saved by his great army;
    a warrior is not delivered by his great strength.
The war horse is a false hope for salvation,
    and by its great might it cannot rescue.
Behold, the eye of the Lord is on those who fear him,
    on those who hope in his steadfast love,
that he may deliver their soul from death
    and keep them alive in famine.
Our soul waits for the Lord;
    he is our help and our shield.
For our heart is glad in him,
    because we trust in his holy name.
Let your steadfast love, O Lord, be upon us,
    even as we hope in you.
Psalm 33:16–22

Imagine all the battles the authors of these psalms had seen and probably won. The temptation would be to trust in your own strength and power. But we're reminded again and again to trust in God above all else. Above chariots, bows, and armies, but also above institutions that are supposed to have the power to save us, like our government and church. As we see throughout the Old Testament, God has power over governments and rulers. There is no one more powerful than He is. And many of us have been hurt by churches we've attended. As a pastor's wife, I've been hurt more deeply by the church than most, but that fuels my love for God. He takes broken, hurting people, puts them together in a church family, and continues to work in them and through them, but not so they get credit for all they can do, but to point to His might.

We may also try to put our faith in doctors and therapists. If we could just get an appointment with the best in the area, all our problems would be solved. In Mark 5, we meet a woman who had tried to find relief from many doctors: "And there was a woman who had had a discharge of blood for twelve years, and who had suffered much under many physicians, and had spent all that she had, and was no better but rather grew worse" (vv. 25–26).

We can so relate! Like so many of us who have tried doctors, therapies, supplements, diets, and tests, this woman was weary. No one could help her. And her issue wasn't just a physical one. Because she was constantly bleeding, she was considered unclean. According to Levitical law, she would have to stay away from others, including her family.

But she had heard reports of Jesus. She knew His reputation as a healer. She was desperate enough to risk touching others and being shamed to get close enough. "For she said, 'If I touch even his garments, I will be made well.' And immediately the flow of blood dried up, and she felt in her body that she was healed of her disease" (vv. 28–29). Relief at last! No more blood. No more loneliness. No more weariness.

She likely tried to sneak away through the crowd as unnoticed as she came, but "Jesus, perceiving in himself that power had gone out from him, immediately turned about in the crowd and said, 'Who touched my garments?'" (v. 30). The disciples looked around, confused. They were sure many people had touched Jesus as they all pressed in on Him. But the woman came forward, fell at His feet, and told Him the whole truth.

We assume when Mark writes "the whole truth" that this woman told Christ about the doctors, about the abuse, about losing all her money, about losing her connections to her family and community. We can imagine her saying, "I went here and there. I saw this doctor and that one. And finally I was without options. So I risked what little I had left to touch you."

And Jesus said to her, "Daughter, your faith has made you well; go in peace, and be healed of your disease" (v. 34). Do you notice what healed her? Jesus said it was her faith! Her faith encouraged her to not give up. Her faith pushed her through that crowd. Her faith gave her the strength to reach out and touch Jesus's robe. And her faith also made her brave enough to come forward when He looked for her in the crowd. Her faith in Him brought relief.

It's interesting to note what Jesus commended in this woman. It wasn't her steadfastness. It wasn't her determination. It wasn't her willingness to elbow herself through the crowd. It was her faith.

When we have meetings about James, I bring a binder full of information. Copies of therapy evaluations, results of blood tests, a list of medicines and supplements, his individualized education program (IEP), and more. It is obvious to others that we are serious about helping him thrive. That we want him to reach his potential. That we take our care for him seriously. Like this woman, we have been to many doctors and therapists and have spent lots of money. Some of these doctors have helped and others haven't. But we continue to have faith.

What is our faith in? The medical community? The most recent study? The newest therapy trend? To a degree, yes. Or we wouldn't keep going there for answers.

But Hebrews 11:1 says, "Now faith is the assurance of things hoped for, the conviction of things not seen." We hope for James to feel better. We can't see it, but we hope for it. And ultimately, our hope is in Christ.

Even if we don't see healing and relief this side of heaven, we continue to have hope in Christ. As John Piper said, "The deepest need that you and I have in weakness and adversity is not quick relief, but the well-grounded confidence that what is happening to us is part of the greatest purpose of God in the universe—the glorification of the grace and power of his Son—the grace and power that bore him to the cross and kept him there until the work of love was done."[2]

In this chapter we talked about what we need to let go of, like our beliefs about God, and what we need to hold on to, who He truly is and our faith in Him. False gospels and false hope try to push us down, but God comes to us as He did to Mary Magdalene and Elijah—showing us who He truly is and how deep His love is for us.

Pete Wilson writes, "One day, everything we hope for will eventually disappoint us. Every circumstance, every situation, every relationship we put our hope in is going to wear out, give out, fall apart, melt down, and go away."[3] What's left? Everything we've ever needed—God Himself.

To Discuss or Journal

1. What changes or necessary adjustments in your life are you trying to accept or deal with?
2. Can you relate to the lies about God that can especially influence special-needs families?
3. Mary Magdalene and Elijah were surprised by how God expanded their ideas about Him and His character. Are there old ways of thinking you've been holding on to? What new lessons are you learning?
4. Have you been putting your faith in substitutes for God? How has this chapter reminded you to go to Him first?
5. Does it bring you comfort or fear to realize everything will fail but God? Why?

three

Where Can I Go?
(Cycles of Grief)

Seeing that a Pilot steers the ship in which we sail, who will
never allow us to perish even in the midst of shipwrecks, there
is no reason why our minds should be overwhelmed with fear
and overcome with weariness.

John Calvin

In 1969, Elisabeth Kübler-Ross introduced the stages of dying
in her book, *On Death and Dying*. Before her death, she and
her new coauthor David Kessler adapted the stages for those
grieving the death of someone they love. The stages are denial,
anger, bargaining, depression, and acceptance. The stages are
well-known now and referenced in books and movies. They
vary in intensity for each person. Those prone to anger may stay
in that stage longer, or those prone to depression may feel stuck
there. Those who aren't comfortable with any of these strong
emotions may try to suppress them all and rush through. But

as author and pastor Peter Scazzero reminds us, "To feel is to be human. To minimize or deny what we feel is a distortion of what it means to be image bearers of our personal God. To the degree that we are unable to express our emotion, we remain impaired in our ability to love God, others, and ourselves well."[1]

On Paul's ship, the sailors didn't want to deal with their suffering. They tried to avoid and ignore it. In Acts 27, we read they were seeking escape and came up with a deceptive plan. But Paul said to them, "Unless these men stay in the ship, you cannot be saved" (v. 31). So they cut away the ropes of the ship's boat, and let it go (see v. 32). Unless you walk through these stages, you won't find healing. When you get a diagnosis for your child, you will likely go through the stages of grief. Like me, you may find these stages are cyclical, and you revisit them at unexpected times. But there is hope both when you are experiencing them for the first time and when you feel the emotions again and again.

Setting Examples for Us to Follow

Jesus Himself worked through most of the stages of grief as He prayed on the Mount of Olives before His own death. Although we don't really see Him in denial since He knew this was the task He came to earth to accomplish, He cycled through the other stages.

- Anger: His anger was directed toward the disciples, who slept when He asked them to keep watch (see Mark 14:37).
- Bargaining: "Abba, Father, all things are possible for you. Remove this cup from me" (Mark 14:36).
- Depression: "My soul is very sorrowful, even to death" (Mark 14:34). "And being in agony he prayed more

earnestly; and his sweat became like great drops of blood falling down to the ground" (Luke 22:44).

- And finally acceptance: "My Father, if this cannot pass unless I drink it, your will be done" (Matthew 26:42).

We know He is our sinless Savior, so we can learn from this example. We see these stages aren't bad or wrong. They are part of healing. Christ sympathizes with us. He has mercy on us. He gives us grace as we move through our pain and hopefully closer to Him.

> Since then we have a great high priest who has passed through the heavens, Jesus, the Son of God, let us hold fast our confession. For we do not have a high priest who is unable to sympathize with our weaknesses, but one who in every respect has been tempted as we are, yet without sin. Let us then with confidence draw near to the throne of grace, that we may receive mercy and find grace to help in time of need.
>
> Hebrews 4:14–16

Not only did Jesus grieve, but we see the stages in the life of David as well. My husband often preaches on the trials we all face. He says we have two choices in suffering: walk with God or walk away from God. When I find myself in a valley, I ask myself, *Will I let this draw me closer to Him or push me away?* David made the decision to grow closer to God through his grief in 2 Samuel, when the prophet Nathan told him the son born to Bathsheba would die:

> David therefore sought God on behalf of the child. And David fasted and went in and lay all night on the ground. And the elders of his house stood beside him, to raise him from the ground, but he would not, nor did he eat food with them. On the seventh day the child died. And the servants of David were

49

afraid to tell him that the child was dead, for they said, "Behold, while the child was yet alive, we spoke to him, and he did not listen to us. How then can we say to him the child is dead? He may do himself some harm." But when David saw that his servants were whispering together, David understood that the child was dead. And David said to his servants, "Is the child dead?" They said, "He is dead." Then David arose from the earth and washed and anointed himself and changed his clothes. And he went into the house of the Lord and worshiped. He then went to his own house. And when he asked, they set food before him, and he ate. Then his servants said to him, "What is this thing that you have done? You fasted and wept for the child while he was alive; but when the child died, you arose and ate food." He said, "While the child was still alive, I fasted and wept, for I said, 'Who knows whether the Lord will be gracious to me, that the child may live?' But now he is dead. Why should I fast? Can I bring him back again? I shall go to him, but he will not return to me."

12:16–23

In this passage we see David go through bargaining, depression, and finally acceptance. At the end, he had faith in God and moved forward, not without sorrow over the son he lost, but with God's grace and mercy in his sorrow. We make the choice like David did to accept our circumstances and learn from them or let our anger, resentment, and frustration drive a wedge between us and the God who calls us to Himself.

Bear with One Another

It's one thing to read about Jesus and David going through the stages of grief, but when you and your spouse are struggling through, there are even more lessons we can learn. The stages of grief are personal and patient—the steps and time frame are different for each person. There is no shame in taking longer than your spouse or another friend to move through them after a diagnosis or any significant life change. The key is being patient with yourself and your loved ones who are also processing the information.

After James's diagnosis, Lee was working through the first stages of grief while I had moved through them and was already in attack mode. I read books. I did internet searches. I had new solutions each day. I remember one conversation we had about diet changes I wanted to implement for James. Two books I had read suggested that going dairy-free and gluten-free could be helpful. I wanted to try it. So I told Lee one night, "We're taking James off of dairy. I think it will help." He had lots of questions.

"Doesn't he need milk? His favorite foods have cheese, like quesadillas and pizza. What else will he eat? What exactly will taking him off dairy accomplish? Does it work for all kids or just some? I'm not sure about this; can we think about it some more?"

"Read the books if you want to know all the answers. I don't have time to wait for you to figure out what I already know," I said. I told him when we got back from visiting my parents for Thanksgiving we were going to make the diet changes (whether he liked it or not). Now that I understand better how we processed James's diagnosis differently, I wish I had shown more patience and grace. At the time I felt like all the pressure was on me to get James as much help as possible as quickly as possible. Thankfully, God worked on both of us that Thanksgiving. (I was also humbled a few months later when Lee and I talked about the diet we attempted. Although it helps some kids on the spectrum, it didn't help James.)

The boys and I flew to Texas a few days ahead of Lee. On the coffee table I left a book I had just finished, *Not My Boy* by Rodney Peete, whose son has autism. When we picked up Lee at the airport he had tears in his eyes. He read the book during the entire three-hour flight. He said, "I get it. I'm in. Whatever we have to do to help him, we'll do." Rodney Peete's honest story of his struggle to accept his son's autism diagnosis made an impact on Lee.

Peete wrote that while his wife was taking their son to therapists' appointments, he was at the bar. His wife, Holly, essentially told him, "Get on board with what we're doing or get out." Rodney changed and became an advocate for his son. In *Louder Than Words*, Jenny McCarthy also discusses her husband's difficulty processing their son's autism diagnosis and the changes that came as a result. Her husband would ignore their son's diet restrictions and not help with therapy at home. Jenny McCarthy and her husband divorced.

We are called to bear with one another in stressful times like these. Paul writes, "I therefore, a prisoner for the Lord, urge you to walk in a manner worthy of the calling to which you have been called, with all humility and gentleness, with patience, bearing with one another in love, eager to maintain the unity of the Spirit in the bond of peace" (Ephesians 4:1–3). We bear with one another, not against each other. It's a lesson Lee and I learned in those first months and continue to apply to our relationship.

A couple years ago we went through a scary experience, and I was the one too stunned and scared to act. I noticed James had blood in his underwear when he came home from school. This happened for a few days over a couple weeks. He also started self-injurious behaviors. I didn't know what to do. I hoped everything was okay and wanted to just ignore it. But we were afraid he might have been a victim of abuse. I couldn't put my worries into words without sobbing, so Lee took the lead. He called a teacher friend to ask advice. That friend was a mandatory reporter and thought there was enough evidence to call child protective services. Lee also called the school and asked for a meeting, telling them James would not return until we resolved the issue. We took James to the emergency room to see a sexual assault nurse examiner. They called the police, as is the policy for this type of case.

With all of their help, we determined James was not being abused in the way we feared. His diaper rash was bleeding when he was being helped with toileting at school. Lee was able to step up when I couldn't. I'm glad we trusted our intuition to find out the truth.

One key is to give yourself and each other lots of grace. There is no shame in what you're feeling. I occasionally get emails from readers of Key Ministry, a website I run for special-needs families. "This post starts off depressing. Can't the writer get over it and move on?" I write back and explain that our hope is to make sure no parent feels alone, no matter what emotion he or she is experiencing. Yes, we always point to the hope we have through Christ, but we never shame a person for how they are feeling in that moment. My parents set such a good example of this for me as I grew up and dealt with the realities of having a sister with Down syndrome. In high school she would embarrass me by telling someone at school something I had talked about at home, assuming it would be kept a secret. My parents didn't start off their response to my anger with "Well, you know she can't help it. . . ." They first said they were sorry it happened and understood how embarrassed I must feel. Then we got to the point of understanding her abilities and motivations (she didn't understand it would embarrass me and she certainly didn't do it with mean intent—which can't be said of embarrassing situations with typical siblings, as I knew from situations with our younger sister!).

Feeling supported and validated when we share our feelings, even the hard ones, should be true in our families, our churches, and in the friendships we look to for support.

In *Trauma and Resilience: A Handbook*, Frauke and Charles Schaefer write:

Acknowledging and voicing uncomfortable emotions is essential for dealing constructively with trauma-related distress. Unfortunately, that is not a characteristic of all present-day conservative Christian churches or organizations. There may be expectations that those who are "right with Christ" and have "enough faith" do not have negative feelings. Consequently, people expressing sorrow, pain, sadness, doubt, or anger (in the American context often described as "negative" emotions) can attract disapproval or even condemnation from fellow believers.[2]

Jesus doesn't condemn us for feeling a full range of emotions, and we shouldn't condemn each other. It's okay to not be okay. There is grace to meet you there. As Ed Welch writes, "Emotional suffering needs spiritual encouragement."[3] That's what we offer each other instead of judgment. Like my parents, who started with empathy and then moved to finding the truth together, we can all take time for kindness before we race into correction. This is true as we go through the stages of grief and as we continue to grow in godliness.

Chronic Grief and PTSD

There are the stages of grief everyone experiences, and then there are cases of deeper grief, which include chronic grief and post-traumatic stress disorder (PTSD).

Chronic grief is grief that doesn't leave you. It is intense and unrelenting. You may read about the cycles of grief you're supposed to move through and wonder about the "moving through" part. You feel stuck. Different from revisiting points of the grief cycle (which we'll discuss in the next section), you never feel like you leave chronic grief. It's a permanent weight on your back, pulling you under the waves again and again as you try to swim on.

PTSD is a mental health issue people experience after an especially traumatic life event. It is often associated with soldiers who return home from combat or victims of assault. PTSD is physical as well as physiological. Your body and your mind react to triggering situations.

If you feel like you are dealing with chronic grief or PTSD, I encourage you to find help. Start by asking your pastor or someone at your church if they recommend a counselor or mental health professional in your area. Ask your physician for a recommendation. If that sounds overwhelming, ask your spouse or a close friend to help you. Lee and I both benefited from grief counseling, and our older son David also did play therapy so he could talk about his grief and anxiety. Lee experienced panic attacks and depression so deep he was helped by medicine in addition to therapy for a time.

Don't let shame or embarrassment keep you from getting the help you need. As Tim Keller writes in *Walking with God through Pain and Suffering*:

> Look at Jesus. He was perfect, right? And yet he goes around crying all the time. He is always weeping, a man of sorrows. Do you know why? Because he is *perfect*. Because when you are not all absorbed in yourself, you can feel the sadness of the world. And therefore, what you actually have is that the joy of the Lord happens inside the sorrow. It doesn't come after the sorrow. It doesn't come after the uncontrollable weeping. The weeping drives you into the joy, it enhances the joy, and then the joy enables you to actually feel your grief without it sinking you. In other words, you are finally emotionally healthy.[4]

Cycles of Grief

"You're being too hard on yourselves," our grief counselor said as Lee and I sat across from her during our first session together. "The cycles of grief aren't linear. You can't check off each stage and move on. They are cyclical. You'll experience them over and over, and likely when you least expect it." We found C. S. Lewis's words to be true: "Part of every misery is, so to speak, the misery's shadow or reflection: the fact that you don't merely suffer but have to keep on thinking about the fact that you suffer."[5]

That made sense for us and seemed like it would be true for other special-needs parents I know. I asked my friends what grief experiences had snuck up on them lately. They said:

- When my six-year-old nephew who is only six weeks younger than my son read me a book. My son struggles to approximate any word.
- My daughter is ten and nonverbal, and she was so upset over something this past weekend. I couldn't help her. She was trying really hard to communicate, and I just didn't know what to do. Sometimes I feel like she's slipping away from me, and I don't know how to bring her back. I feel absolutely helpless. After that moment, I just cried and cried.
- It hits me at the weirdest times. My son has high functioning Asperger's. Like when he comes out of the junior high alone at pickup and every one else walks out talking and goofing with their friends. When he acts younger than his age at church and all the other kids his age are helping and listening to the service. When my ten-year-old says "Mom, why can't he act like other big brothers!?"
- My youngest is going to be graduating in May and is excitedly making plans to go off to college. My twenty-year-old son with autism is home full time now, and I need a caregiver if I want to do anything. It's hard thinking of how different Alex's life could be if he weren't autistic.

- Things hit me out of the blue all the time too . . . most recently was Valentine's Day watching the children at his school excitedly exchange handmade cards and candy. Sounds petty but it was just another reminder of something my precious guy isn't able to be a part of yet.
- Every single time I hear a child say "Mama" . . . How I *long* to hear that one day from my son.

Each of us could tell stories of surprising grief. By far, the hardest day of our entire first year of James's autism diagnosis was his first day of school. Even though I had worked through the initial stages of grief after his diagnosis, on this day I went through all five stages of grief in one afternoon. My idols failed and fell. God gently but firmly placed Himself in the middle of my mess and redeemed it. It was a turning point for me.

On that first day of school, just weeks after getting James's diagnosis, we stood outside in the snow at 12:30 p.m. waiting for his new teacher, therapists, and aides to walk him through the front doors. We took lots of pictures and pretended we were excited. But I was heartbroken. Lee went on to work and David and I came home. I went into the bathroom and shut the door. I told God the whole truth. I didn't want my child to have autism. I didn't want to take him to a public elementary school when he was only three years old. I really didn't want to take him to the special-education class. I didn't want to know the names of any therapists. No IEPs. No paperwork. I wanted to homeschool him like I homeschooled his brother. I wanted our home to be enough. *I wanted to be enough.*

Pastor Pete Wilson writes, "I think for those of us in the midst of a Plan B we'll discover that one of our idols all along has been a picture of the way life should be. Our idol was an expectation or a dream."[6] That certainly described me. I was angry at God because my life was not going according to my plan. Again I struggled with the sin of entitlement.

I called Lee but he didn't answer. I called my mom but she didn't answer. It was just me and God in the bathroom that afternoon. After moving through denial, anger, bargaining, and depression, I finally calmed down by reminding myself, "God loves me; God loves James."

Eventually I came out of the bathroom. I went back to school to pick up James. His teacher said he was sad on and off, but that overall he'd had a very good first day. Even in my grief, I was thankful. We were going to have to adjust to our new normal, and I would continue to learn how grief can sneak up and surprise you.

The stages of grief take time to move through and hit again and again, but not even time heals like God Himself does. When I run up against the wall of grief, I open the Bible to the Psalms. Psalm 107 is my favorite. Look with me at the hope it presents:

- For those who are lonely and have no place to call home, He "satisfies the longing soul, and the hungry soul he fills with good things" (v. 9).
- For those in darkness, in the shadow of death, He "brought them out of darkness and the shadow of death, and burst their bonds apart" (v. 14).
- For those who were fools and suffered affliction, He "sent out his word and healed them, and delivered them from their destruction" (v. 20).

And the part I relate to most, to those who were going down in ships (those of us on a ride we didn't know we had signed up for!):

Then they cried to the Lord in their trouble,
and he delivered them from their distress.

He made the storm be still,
  and the waves of the sea were hushed.
Then they were glad that the waters were quiet,
  and he brought them to their desired haven.
Let them thank the Lord for his steadfast love,
  for his wondrous works to the children of man!
Let them extol him in the congregation of the people,
  and praise him in the assembly of the elders.

vv. 28–32

We can follow this pattern when grief threatens to engulf us. We can cry out. We can experience the peace He brings to our circumstances (even if the circumstances don't change). We can thank Him for His love. We can praise Him with others.

When Paul experienced grief and pain due to a "thorn in the flesh," he used it as an opportunity to teach those at the church in Corinth:

Three times I pleaded with the Lord about this, that it should leave me. But he said to me, "My grace is sufficient for you, for my power is made perfect in weakness." Therefore I will boast all the more gladly of my weaknesses, so that the power of Christ may rest upon me. For the sake of Christ, then, I am content with weaknesses, insults, hardships, persecutions, and calamities. For when I am weak, then I am strong.

2 Corinthians 12:8–10

Pastor Scazzero points out, "The strength he received from Christ was not the strength to change, deny, or defy his circumstances; it was the strength to be content in the midst of them, to surrender to God's loving will for him."[7]

Wherever you are in the cycles of grief right now, know there is hope. Even if you are like me and experience that cycle of grief over and over again. Each time we feel ourselves going down with the sorrow ship, we know God will meet us there and offer the hand of hope.

To Discuss or Journal

1. Had you heard about the stages of grief before reading this chapter? What has your experience been with them?

2. Have you noticed a difference in the ways you and your spouse or other close family members have responded to the news of having a child with a disability?

3. We see from the examples of Jesus and David that our emotions aren't wrong and shouldn't be ignored. Do you tend to be comfortable with strong emotions or not? If not, how has reading about the examples from this chapter encouraged you to know it's okay not to be okay?

4. If you feel like you are experiencing chronic grief or PTSD, do you have a plan for getting more help? Ask your group leader or pastor for resources.

5. Have you experienced the cyclical nature of grief? When has it snuck up on you? What brings you hope in those moments?

four

What We Overcome in Order to Move On

Guilt, Fear, Shame

Suffering is unbearable if you aren't certain that God is for you and with you.

Timothy Keller

Just as we are not the first people to suffer, we are also not the first to experience the emotions that seem to drive our actions and reactions. Each one of us struggles with guilt, fear, or shame. We even see each of these reactions to the first sin in the Garden of Eden.

Genesis chapter 3 gives an account of the first sin: disobeying God's command not to eat the fruit of the tree in the midst of the garden. When Adam and Eve gave in to Satan's temptation, their eyes were opened and the burden of knowledge was put on them. As Tim Challies writes, "No sooner do they sin than they experience *shame*, symbolized in the sudden knowledge that they are naked and their desire to cover themselves. They experience *fear* as they run and hide from God, desperate to escape his gaze. They experience *guilt*, knowing that they have gone from innocent to guilty in the eyes of God."[1]

But the gospel is good news to those of us carrying the burdens of guilt, fear, and shame. Just as the sailors on Paul's journey had to lighten their loads in order to survive (see Acts 27:38), we must let go of the overwhelming responses that are dragging us down.

Guilt

A few years ago James and I sat down at a potluck our church was having with another church. Potlucks aren't easy for us, especially as the pastor's family. Lee needs to be free to talk to everyone, which means I'm on my own with the boys. In line, James grabs at the foods he wants, and I can't balance our plates while dishing out the food and keeping his hands out of the desserts. So by the time we sat down at a table on that day, I was already a little on edge, especially because I didn't know the members of this church and they didn't know James. Since autism is invisible, people have the expectation that he is a typical child. It doesn't take long for them to figure out he isn't typical.

The lady across from us at the table gestured to James and asked, "Is he going to grow out of that?" I wasn't sure what she meant. "His autism? Will he grow out of his autism?" "Yes," she answered. Then followed up with, "What did you do when you were pregnant to make him that way?"

What did I do to make him that way? Well, there are lots of theories. Decades ago autism in children was blamed on the "refrigerator mother theory." In 1943, when psychiatrist Leo Kanner first identified autism, he noted the lack of warmth among the parents of autistic children, especially their mothers. In a 1949 paper, he wrote that autism may be related to a "genuine lack of maternal warmth," noted that fathers rarely stepped down to indulge in children's play, and observed that children were exposed from "the beginning to parental coldness, obsessiveness, and a mechanical type of attention to material needs only. . . . They were left neatly in refrigerators which did not defrost. Their withdrawal seems to be an act of turning away from such a situation to seek comfort in solitude."[2] In a 1960 interview, Kanner bluntly described parents of autistic children as "just happening to defrost enough to produce a child."[3]

Some theories still blame mothers for autism. In another conversation I had with a mom at my older son's theater rehearsal I was asked, "Did you eat a lot of tuna when you were pregnant? I hear that's what causes those problems." There are vaccines, pollution, and chemical causes (like getting your hair dyed while pregnant), and the list goes on and on. The questions doctors and therapists ask when doing intake forms don't help ease the guilt we feel: What medicines did I take when pregnant? How long was I in labor? Did I have an epidural? How many ear infections did he have as a child? What antibiotics did he take? Every answer makes me question each decision I made from the moment I knew I was pregnant with him.

To be clear, we don't fully understand what leads to autism, so the answers to every one of these questions may not matter at all. But when you're vulnerable, when you're scared, when everyone from your great-aunt who read some article about autism in her magazine to your pediatrician seems to think you had something to do with it, you feel the heavy burden of guilt.

Guilt can be healthy. The conviction of the Holy Spirit can bring feelings of guilt or remorse over sin and lead you to repentance. But I'm talking about the guilt that causes you to always relive the past, to carry that remorse into your daily life. Let's look at how Jesus reacted to a woman carrying the heavy burden of guilt and her reaction after meeting Him.

In John 4, Jesus and His disciples traveled through Samaria, a place usually avoided by Jews. Verse 9 tells us, "Jews have no dealings with Samaritans." But verse 4 tells us, "He *had* to pass through Samaria" (emphasis added), so there He was, sitting near a well, exhausted from His journey. With His disciples off buying food in the city, He was alone when a woman approached to draw water from the well. Most women came earlier in the day when it was cooler. He asked her to give Him a drink:

> The Samaritan woman said to him, "How is it that you, a Jew, ask for a drink from me, a woman of Samaria?" (For Jews have no dealings with Samaritans.) Jesus answered her, "If you knew the gift of God, and who it is that is saying to you, 'Give me a drink,' you would have asked him, and he would have given you living water." The woman said to him, "Sir, you have nothing to draw water with, and the well is deep. Where do you get that living water? Are you greater than our father Jacob? He gave us the well and drank from it himself, as did his sons and his livestock." Jesus said to her, "Everyone who drinks of this water will be thirsty again, but whoever drinks of the water that I will give him will never be thirsty again. The water that I will give him will become in him a spring of water welling up to eternal life." The woman said to him, "Sir, give me this water, so that I will not be thirsty or have to come here to draw water."
>
> John 4:9–15

But then the conversation takes a turn from focusing on Jesus to focusing on her.

> Jesus said to her, "Go, call your husband, and come here." The woman answered him, "I have no husband." Jesus said to her, "You are right in saying, 'I have no husband'; for you have had five husbands, and the one you now have is not your husband. What you have said is true." The woman said to him, "Sir, I perceive that you are a prophet."
>
> vv. 16–19

She was likely racked with guilt at this moment, and tried to turn the conversation away from herself, to a topic she knew a Jew would have a strong opinion about:

> "Our fathers worshiped on this mountain, but you say that in Jerusalem is the place where people ought to worship." Jesus said to her, "Woman, believe me, the hour is coming when neither on this mountain nor in Jerusalem will you worship the Father. You worship what you do not know; we worship what we know, for salvation is from the Jews. But the hour is coming, and is now here, when the true worshipers will worship the Father in spirit and truth, for the Father is seeking such people to worship him. God is spirit, and those who worship him must worship in spirit and truth." The woman said to him, "I know that Messiah is coming (he who is called Christ). When he comes, he will tell us all things." Jesus said to her, "I who speak to you am he."
>
> vv. 20–26

As the disciples came back and questioned what Jesus was doing, Scripture tells us, "So the woman left her water jar and went away into town and said to the people, 'Come, see a man who told me all that I ever did. Can this be the Christ?'" (vv. 28–29). How did the town respond to this woman who carried so much guilt, she hid from them by drawing water when she wouldn't have to see them?

> Many Samaritans from that town believed in him because of the woman's testimony, "He told me all that I ever did." So when the Samaritans came to him, they asked him to stay with them, and he stayed there two days. And many more believed because of his word. They said to the woman, "It is no longer because of what you said that we believe, for we have heard for ourselves, and we know that this is indeed the Savior of the world."
>
> vv. 39–42

One meeting with Christ, that's all it took to free her from the guilt she carried. And once she was free, she didn't live in the past anymore. She could face the townspeople with her new confidence in what Christ had done. Even if she sat at a table across from someone who said, "Aren't you that woman . . . ?" she could reply, "Let me tell you what I know now . . ." And we can follow her example. What vaccines did you give him? How much tuna did you eat? Did you live in a city with high pollution? None of the answers to those questions matter as much as pointing people to the hope we have in Christ now.

"For I know the plans I have for you, declares the Lord, plans for welfare and not for evil, to give you a future and a hope. Then you will call upon me and come and pray to me, and I will hear you. You will seek me and find me, when you seek me with all your heart" (Jeremiah 29:11–13). Walk away from guilt and toward the future and hope Christ provides!

Fear

Ask one hundred special-needs parents what their number one stress is and it's likely most of them will answer, "The unknown future for my kids." And it can hit us at each stage of development. What happens when he moves from preschool to grade school? What happens when she's too old to receive treatment at the pediatric hospital? What will he do after he graduates? Who will care for her when we're gone?

In 2015, *Dateline* set out to answer one of the questions that often plagues us: What happens when those with special needs age out of the education system? They spent three years following two families with young adult sons on the autism spectrum. Even the promo sounds ominous: "Graduation is supposed to be a joyful time for families, but mothers Lenore Kubicsko and Mary Clancy are filled not only with pride, but also terror and dread as their young adult sons with autism prepare to leave school."[4]

When I asked on my Facebook page if anyone had seen it, one friend said she didn't think she could watch. I saw autism parents on Twitter saying the same thing. Why? Because we're scared. We don't know what's going to happen with our kids when they graduate from high school, and we don't want to even think about it until we have to.

How do we look to the future without fear? The woman described in Proverbs 31 is said to laugh at the time to come (see v. 25). What can we learn from her example? How do we combat the fear that keeps us up at night and steals our joy when we're awake?

The Bible tells us the most powerful weapon against fear: faith in God's love. "There is no fear in love, but perfect love casts out fear" (1 John 4:18).

When we remember how much He loves us, how much He loves our children, it casts out fear.

> For I am sure that neither death nor life, nor angels nor rul-
> ers, nor things present nor things to come, nor powers, nor

height nor depth, nor anything else in all creation, will be able to separate us from the love of God in Christ Jesus our Lord.

Romans 8:38–39

For I know the plans I have for you, declares the Lord, plans for welfare and not for evil, to give you a future and a hope.

Jeremiah 29:11

For you shall not go out in haste,
and you shall not go in flight,
for the Lord will go before you,
and the God of Israel will be your rear guard.

Isaiah 52:12

And my God will supply every need of yours according to his riches in glory in Christ Jesus.

Philippians 4:19

The Proverbs 31 woman doesn't laugh at the time to come because she has it all figured out. She laughs because she has confidence in the One who does.

John Calvin wrote, "When the light of Divine Providence has illuminated the believer's soul, he is relieved and set free, not only from the extreme fear and anxiety, which formerly oppressed him, but from all care."[5]

We see God's care for those in need throughout Scripture. In the last chapter of 1 Samuel, we read about Saul's death and the deaths of his sons Jonathan, Abinadab, and Malchi-shua. David had already been anointed king by Samuel, but had been on the run from Saul, who was jealous and wanted him dead. Earlier, in 1 Samuel 18:8, Saul had said, "They have ascribed to David ten thousands, and to me they have ascribed thousands, and what more can he have but the kingdom?" The next verse says from that day on, Saul eyed David. But David and Saul's son Jonathan became friends. Jonathan warned David when his father was going to attack and said to him, "Go in peace, because we have sworn both of us in the name of the Lord, saying, 'The Lord shall be between me and you, and between my offspring and your offspring, forever'" (1 Samuel 20:42). Even after Jonathan's death, David remembered their vow.

In 2 Samuel chapter 9, David asked, "Is there still anyone left of the house of Saul, that I may show him kindness for Jonathan's sake?" (v. 1). A servant told David, "There is still a son of Jonathan; he is crippled in his feet" (v. 3). If we look back at 2 Samuel 4:4, we see he was crippled because his nurse took him and fled at the news of his father's death. He fell and became lame. Jonathan's son was dependent on others for his care. David asked for Mephibosheth to be brought to him. Mephibosheth came before the king and fell on his face before him. David said to him, "Do not fear, for I will show you kindness for the sake of your father Jonathan, and I will restore to you all the land of Saul your father, and you shall eat at my table always" (2 Samuel 9:7). Verse 11 continues, "So Mephibosheth ate at David's table, like one of the king's sons."

God did not forget Mephibosheth. He did not let David forget either. Mephibosheth probably felt like he was alone and forgotten until David found him, but he never was. Isaiah 50:10 says, "Let him who walks in darkness and has no light trust in the name of the Lord and rely on his God." Even during the darkest times, we don't have to fear because we trust in Him. God knows what strength you will need. He knows the battles you will face. He knows the heartbreak you may feel.

Psalm 34:4 says, "I sought the Lord, and he answered me and delivered me from all my fears." Seek Him today. Listen for His answer. Experience His deliverance. And fear not, not in your present circumstances or your unknown future. God is here and already there, and He cares for you.

Shame

Guilt keeps you in the past. Fear keeps you in the future. But shame is about your present circumstances. Of these three challenges, shame hits me the hardest. Especially on Wednesdays.

"You may want to wear these armguards," Ashley said as we prepared to go in the padded room where James would do his therapy. His anxiety has been increasing over the last year, and because of his limited verbal ability, it often exhibits as aggressive and self-injurious behavior. He hits himself and others (mostly me since I'm with him the most) to express what he can't say. So on Wednesdays we go to a local college with an outstanding autism center with master's-level students who focus on behaviors and communication. Last year we were part of a study on pica (eating nonfood items), and it was successful. So we were eager for more help with this even bigger challenge.

Since I'm the one so often hit, I am much more involved in this therapy. And to figure out why he's hitting, they have to see him do it. So I withhold attention and toys he wants for short, specific amounts of time, and they gather data on how long it takes him to get mad enough to hit me. In the padded room, I turn away from him while watching the cartoon *Backyardigans* on YouTube on my phone. He wants the phone, so he first tries to make eye contact, then he pulls on my arm, then he hits me, himself, or the wall. They write it all down, and we do it again. He gets rewarded for not hitting, gets lots of breaks, and actually loves therapy day, but it is exhausting to me. Not just because I'm getting hit, but because I feel judged.

Brené Brown is a shame researcher and has written extensively on the topic. She shares, "Shame is the intensely painful feeling or experience of believing that we are flawed and therefore unworthy of love and belonging."⁶ It is related to guilt, but different. Guilt says, "I have done something bad." Shame says, "I am bad." So when we go to therapy each Wednesday, I don't just feel like I've *made a mistake* in how I've handled James's aggression up to this point, I feel like *I am the mistake*. I am a bad mom. I am bad.

Like guilt and fear, the gospel has an answer for shame as well. Peter found it when he experienced the deepest shame of his life.

Jesus knew it would happen. As Jesus turned His thoughts to the cross, He and Peter had a conversation.

> Simon Peter said to him, "Lord, where are you going?" Jesus answered him, "Where I am going you cannot follow me now, but you will follow afterward." Peter said to him, "Lord, why can I not follow you now? I will lay down my life for you." Jesus answered, "Will you lay down your life for me? Truly, truly, I say to you, the rooster will not crow till you have denied me three times."
>
> John 13:36–38

It doesn't take long for us to see Jesus's prediction come true:

> Then they seized [Jesus] and led him away, bringing him into the high priest's house, and Peter was following at a distance. And when they had kindled a fire in the middle of the courtyard and sat down together, Peter sat down among them. Then a servant girl, seeing him as he sat in the light and looking closely at him, said, "This man also was with him." But he denied it, saying, "Woman, I do not know him." And a little later someone else saw him and said, "You also are one of them." But Peter said, "Man, I am not." And after an interval of about an hour still another insisted, saying, "Certainly this man also was with him, for he too is a Galilean." But Peter said, "Man, I do not know what you are talking about." And immediately,

while he was still speaking, the rooster crowed. And the Lord turned and looked at Peter. And Peter remembered the saying of the Lord, how he had said to him, "Before the rooster crows today, you will deny me three times." And he went out and wept bitterly.

Luke 22:54–62

Peter had acted exactly as Jesus said he would. And Peter felt that shame. Not just "I made a mistake," but "I am a mistake."

But Jesus is the solution.

When Mary Magdalene and Mary the mother of James and Salome went to Jesus's tomb, they saw a young man in a white robe. "And he said to them, 'Do not be alarmed. You seek Jesus of Nazareth, who was crucified. He has risen; he is not here. See the place where they laid him. But go, tell his disciples and Peter that he is going before you to Galilee. There you will see him, just as he told you'" (Mark 16:6–7). Did you catch the small detail in this verse? *And Peter.* Jesus knew Peter's shame would keep him hidden.

Brené writes, "When we feel shame, we are most likely to protect ourselves by blaming something or someone, rationalizing our lapse, offering a disingenuous apology, or hiding out."[7] But what kills shame is empathy. "If we can share our story with someone who responds with empathy and understanding, shame can't survive."[8]

When Jesus and Peter walked together near the Sea of Tiberias, Peter's shame was healed as Jesus gently reminded him of the truth and gave him a mission. "Do you love me?" Jesus asked, giving Peter the opportunity to say he did. Three times he asked, and the final time Peter responded, "Lord, you know everything; you know that I love you" (John 21:17). Our Savior knows everything. Every secret we try to hide. Every mistake that becomes our identity. He knows, He sees, and He loves us anyway.

The light He brings into our darkness reminds us we are who He says we are, not what shame says we are. Peter himself later wrote, "But you are a chosen race, a royal priesthood, a holy nation, a people for his own possession, that you may proclaim the excellencies of him who called you out of darkness into his marvelous light" (1 Peter 2:9). Meeting Christ pushed away the shame and gave him a new identity. Then he was ready to move on to his purpose—build Christ's church by caring for Christ's people. When we turn the pages in our Bible from the end of the Gospel of John to the book of Acts, we see Peter fulfill the first stages of that mission by preaching at Pentecost.

Shame didn't have the final say in Peter's life, and it doesn't in our lives either. You are more than the mistakes you've made or the weaknesses you feel. His love meets you where you are and gently reminds you of your identity in Him.

To Discuss or Journal

1. Guilt isn't unique to special-needs parents, but we often carry a heavier burden of it than other parents. If you struggle with guilt, share that with your group, spouse, or friends. Know that those feelings don't come from God and He wants you to be free from guilt.

2. We fear many what-if scenarios and possible futures for our family members. But when you look back on your life, can you recall times you had fear and then everything worked out? And even if those situations didn't go as planned, you saw God at work?

3. Shame is believing you are what you do or have done, especially the mistakes you've made. How does reading about Peter release you from feeling shame?

4. Of these three struggles, which one stands out to you most? Living in the past with guilt, living in the future with fear, or living in the present with shame?

5. How does the hope of the gospel meet your deepest need?

five

Hold On

Lucy woke out of the deepest sleep you can imagine, with the feeling that the voice she liked best in the world had been calling her name.

C. S. Lewis, *Prince Caspian*

The cycles of grief affect your mind and heart, but as you suffer and recover, you also need to pay attention to your body. When Paul was adrift at sea, he was aware of the practical needs of those around him. "Therefore I urge you to take some food. For it will give you strength, for not a hair is to perish from the head of any of you" (Acts 27:34). The truth is, you may have felt like you were going to die. But you didn't. And now you need to get back to taking care of yourself. You won't be able to function like you did before, but you can learn new ways to care for yourself.

First Peter 5:10 says, "And after you have suffered a little while, the God of all grace, who has called you to his eternal glory in Christ, will himself restore, confirm, strengthen, and establish you." Did you notice how it starts? With the word *after*. You will suffer, and there will be an after. You need to live in this "after" in new ways, and the promise from Peter is that Christ Himself will restore, confirm, strengthen, and establish you. How did Peter know this was true? He experienced it himself.

Peter and Jesus had a unique relationship. Peter was in Jesus's inner circle of disciples who saw Jesus's transfiguration (see Matthew 17:1–13) and was asked to pray with Jesus on the Mount of Olives before His arrest and betrayal (see Matthew 26:37). Jesus called Peter away from his life as a fisherman (see Matthew 4:18–22), He called him to step out of a boat and walk on water to him (see Matthew 14:28–33), and He entered Peter's house and healed his mother-in-law (see Matthew 8:14–15).

Even through their years together, Jesus knew Peter better than Peter knew himself. As we read in the previous chapter, He predicted Peter's denial during Christ's trial.

I can't image how Peter suffered through the events that followed: the trials of Jesus, hearing the crowd yell "Crucify him," seeing Him mocked and tortured, and finally the crucifixion and Christ's death. Oh, the weight of disappointment Peter must have felt! And to believe he wouldn't have the opportunity to prove himself again.

We read in each gospel account about Jesus appearing to disciples and followers after His resurrection, but it's John who tells us about Peter's restoration with Christ. Peter would likely remember this conversation years later, as he wrote that Christ will "himself restore, confirm, strengthen, and establish you." Peter knew firsthand the power of this process.

After the disciples suffered through His death and tried to understand His resurrection, Jesus did two very important things: He fed them and He gave them a new purpose. On the same beach where Jesus and Peter walked and talked, He had said to them all, "Come and have breakfast" as He "took the bread and gave it to them, and so with the fish" (John 21:12–13). Jesus reminded them to meet their physical needs and then sent them out on a mission. And He will do the same for you as He leads you to restoration after you have suffered.

Caring for yourself during this time is so important. You have to remember to breathe, eat, and sleep, so you can live out your Plan B purpose.

Breathe

When you feel like you're drowning, even breathing can be hard. One day when I was about seven years old my family went to a friend's house to swim. My older sister, Syble, was eight and playing independently in her life jacket near my dad, who held our toddler sister, Sarah, in his arms. Mom was close by reading a book in the shade. The pool had a hot tub next to it, with a bench all the way around to sit on. It didn't look that deep to me, so I snapped off my life jacket and climbed onto the bench, enjoying the rush of the jets. Then I decided to step off toward the middle. I could see the drain at the bottom clearly and thought I could stand there and keep my head above water. But it was much deeper than I realized. I sank to the bottom, kicked myself back up as hard as I could, and yelled for my mom. Then I gasped for air, sank again, kicked up, and yelled when I hit the surface of the water. I'm sure this only happened a couple times before my mom rushed over and pulled me out, although to my seven-year-old self, it seemed to take forever. Each time I could take a breath, it left me just as quickly as it came. I remember how desperate I felt for my mom to save me. To this day I can't swim. I can hold my nose with my fingers and go under water for a few seconds, but then I remember what it feels like not to be able to breathe, and I pop up as quickly as I can.

How do I face my biggest fear? How do I keep it from paralyzing me when we pack up the car and drive forty-five minutes down to the gulf coast to enjoy the ocean? I put my faith in the One the winds and the waves obey. "When the waters saw you, O God, when the waters saw you, they were afraid; indeed, the deep trembled" (Psalm 77:16).

The fact that you woke up this morning to breathe in and out all day long is proof God has a purpose for you. That breath is the first gift you receive from Him each morning. Some of you may struggle with panic attacks that cause you to feel like you can't catch your breath. Your heart races and you feel weak or dizzy. The harder you try to calm yourself down, the harder it is for you to calm down. Or you wake up in the middle of the night panting and sweating because fear or worry has hijacked your sleep and your subconscious mind can't battle against it without your conscious help.

Our older son has struggled at times with fear and anxiety. It happens most often at bedtime. We came up with a phrase to say as he inhales and exhales to help him breathe when he feels like he can't: "God loves me" (said or thought while inhaling); "God is for me" (said or thought while exhaling). "God loves me; God is for me"—over and over again until he believes it. Breathing brings us out of negative thoughts and emotions and back into the reality of life. Your mind imagines the worst-case scenario is right around the corner, but your eyes can see the next step into the light.

The disciples were on a boat one day when Jesus fell asleep. The windstorm came and the boat filled with water. "And they went and woke him, saying, 'Master, Master, we are perishing!'" (Luke 8:24). They couldn't breathe. They were scared for their lives. "And he awoke and rebuked the wind and the raging waves, and they ceased, and there was a calm" (v. 24). Amazed, they said to each other, "Who then is this, that he commands even winds and water, and they obey him?" (v. 25). It's the same Savior who gave you breath this morning and has sustained you all day long.

In the movie *Sleepless in Seattle*, Sam had lost his wife and he was asked how he's going to survive his grief. "Well, I'm gonna get out of bed every morning . . . breathe in and out all day long. Then, after a while I won't have to remind myself to get out of bed every morning and breathe in and out . . . and, then after a while, I won't have to think about how I had it great and perfect for a while."[1] We can do that too by focusing on Psalm 46:10, "Be still, and know that I am God." Taking a breath can help you be still and remember the giver of that breath of air.

Eat

Your tendency in a shipwreck situation may be forgetting to eat. Your tendency may be to eat more than you need. But what is true in either situation is that God cares about your nourishment and strength. Just as Jesus told Peter and the disciples, "Come and have breakfast" as He "took the bread and gave it to them, and so with the fish" (John 21:12–13), Paul shared a meal with the other passengers on his ship: "He took bread, and giving thanks to God in the presence of all he broke it and began to eat. Then they all were encouraged and ate some food themselves" (Acts 27:35–36). The simple act of eating well is important in your self-care.

Jesus spoke often of food. One of His best-known miracles was feeding five thousand people with the meager offering of five loaves and two fish (see Matthew 14). When asked how to pray, He taught His disciples to say, "Give us each day our daily bread" (Luke 11:3). John records His words about Himself: "I am the bread of life; whoever comes to me shall not hunger, and whoever believes in me shall never thirst" (6:35). And at the Last Supper, He set an example we follow today:

> And as they were eating, he took bread, and after blessing it broke it and gave it to them, and said, "Take; this is my body." And he took a cup, and when he had given thanks he gave it to them, and they all drank of it. And he said to them, "This is my blood of the covenant, which is poured out for many. Truly, I say to you, I will not drink again of the fruit of the vine until that day when I drink it new in the kingdom of God."
>
> Mark 14:22–25

Eating reminds us of our dependence on what God provides—on the land to grow crops and on the animals who supply meat. I started gardening when Lee pastored his first church, a congregation of less than thirty people in rural North Carolina. Everyone in our church had a garden, so we decided to do one too. We tilled the land, sowed the seeds, pulled the weeds, prayed for rain, and collected the harvest. At each step we were reminded of God's provision, even into the winter months as we ate what I canned from the garden.

Remember in this season that God wants you to be healthy. He has provided the food you need to remain strong. Thank Him for your daily bread and focus on the good gift of food.

Remember also the blessings of eating with others. Like the disciples on the beach and Paul on the ship, sharing a meal together does more than feed the body, it feeds the soul. When I feel wrecked, the last thing I want is to be around people. I may try to avoid family and friends, I want to stay home from church, and I certainly don't want to have people over. But my extrovert husband often needs people to pull him out of sad times. He reminds me that one of God's sweetest gifts is fellowship with others. So I open myself and my home and never regret it.

Sleep

"We do hard things" was our family motto for years. We used to encourage each other with it when we needed to be brave. We would tease each other with it when one of us didn't want to put away the laundry or take out the trash. But after an especially stressful season, we changed our motto from "We do hard things" to "We take naps." There comes a time to stop pushing yourself and just rest. If you don't do it by choice, you may have to do it by necessity. Some days the bravest thing you can do is put on pants with an elastic waistband and pull the covers over your head.

Sleeping is proof of our humanity and our dependence on God. He designed us to need rest and restoration. To turn it all off for as many hours as we can get. I don't mean it's easy to sleep when you're in shipwreck mode. One night I went to bed and said to God, *As long as these two things don't happen, we will survive this. I'm going to fall asleep trusting in You to keep us from this tragedy.* And you know what? One of those two things did happen the next day. And I had to go to sleep the next night thinking, *Okay, God, You got us through something I didn't think we'd be able to survive. And I'm thankful. But tonight I'll go to sleep again, asking you to work out a miracle while I cease from working and thinking.*

In shipwreck mode, you think if you stop kicking, striving, and reaching, you'll sink deeper and faster. But it's mentally and physically exhausting. You think your survival is up to you, and sleeping is like admitting in a small way it's not. It's a reminder of your humanity and frailty. It's a reminder of your dependence on the One who doesn't sleep. "Behold, he who keeps Israel will neither slumber nor sleep" (Psalm 121:4). This same God watches over you as you sleep. "In peace I will both lie down and sleep; for you alone, O Lord, make me dwell in safety" (Psalm 4:8).

Maybe you know you need to sleep, but turning out the light turns on your mind. And it just won't stop. We say that my husband, Lee, sometimes lives with worry about the future and guilt about the past. It's very hard for him to be in the moment, especially when he wakes up at three in the morning and can't get back to sleep. He reminds himself of the encouragement in Proverbs 3:24: "If you lie down, you will not be afraid; when you lie down, your sleep will be sweet." If it helps you to journal before bed or make a to-do list for the next day so your mind can be at rest, make that part of your routine. Lee and David have started listing three things they are thankful for that happened that day so they remember to stay in the present moment and not dwell on the past or anticipate the future.

Unlike my husband, who is quick to fall asleep but often wakes up in the middle of the night, I struggle to fall asleep. It can take me over an hour to stop tossing and turning. Here's how I've learned to fall asleep faster when it's time. I go to bed and wake up at the same time every day. In bed at nine, asleep by ten. Awake at six, out of bed by six thirty. There are other ways I make falling asleep easier. I don't drink caffeine after noon. You may be able to stop at two or five in the afternoon, but noon works best for me. I turn the computer off at nine in the evening. In fact, I try to avoid anything backlit an hour before bedtime. I read from nine until I'm ready to go to sleep. Most people say they can't read fiction before bed, but I prefer it. It usually doesn't require me to think too much. If I'm not asleep thirty minutes after I've gone to bed, I take melatonin. (I need it maybe once a month.)

We've been through seasons when it isn't worry or the fear of giving up control that is keeping us from sleeping—it's James. He goes through phases of waking up at two or three in the morning and staying awake until bedtime the next night. There was even one night when he slept from eight to ten and then woke up and stayed awake all night long. We were visiting Lee's parents and I felt stuck in the room we were in so we didn't wake up anyone else. It was awful. I was begging God for sleep. I know how stressful those seasons are, and I wish I could make them easier for all of us. Instead I pray for supernatural energy to meet my family's needs and for the seasons of sleeplessness to be as short as possible. A lack of sleep can make everything seem harder than it actually is, which is especially bad for shipwreck mode, but we can't control the sleep we get or don't get when our kids are the ones keeping us up. Remain aware of your emotions and other triggers when you're exhausted and turn them over to God to help you work through.

God Will Restore

Remember again the words of Peter, that after you suffer, Christ will "restore, confirm, strengthen, and establish you." In the book of Joel, God promises His people "I will restore to you the years that the swarming locust has eaten" (2:25). There is no wasted time with God. No matter how depleted and "eaten" you may feel, God will work to restore you as you breathe, eat, and sleep. These basics of self-care will help you move forward to fulfill your mission from God—to care for the family He has given you and make a difference in the lives of others.

To Discuss or Journal

1. How has your grief affected you physically?
2. Have you experienced a time when it felt hard to breathe? How does that memory affect you during times of stress?
3. Whether you tend to overeat or not eat enough, how does thinking about how much God cares for your nourishment change your perspective?
4. Getting enough sleep can be a struggle for many reasons. If you are in a sleepless season, what is the cause? Would the practical tips in this chapter work for you?
5. How does reading about how God will restore this time bring you comfort?

six

Adjust Your Routines

How we spend our days is, of course, how we spend our lives.
What we do with this hour, and that one, is what we are doing.

Annie Dillard, *The Writing Life*

In our fourteen-year marriage, we've moved seven times—including a move from North Carolina to Pennsylvania and a move from Pennsylvania to Texas. We've lived in houses, parsonages, town houses, and a mobile home. Each time I stand in the middle of all the packed boxes we have to load onto the waiting truck, I wonder where it all came from.

We recently moved again, and I went from my biggest kitchen ever to the smallest. In the house we rented for two years before our recent move, we had so much extra room in the kitchen we used the top shelves of all the cabinets to hold books. In my kitchen now, I have three drawers. Even with all the purging I've done for each move, going from ten drawers to three is a big change. I had to decide what was most important to have within easy reach (the cheese grater for James's daily quesadillas) and what could be stored somewhere else (the chopsticks none of us can really use anyway).

I think it's important to discuss real life, practical steps we can take when we feel like so much is out of our control, so I've made this chapter full of practical steps I've taken to make big events like moving day *and* regular days easier to manage.

Your Plan B Life Needs Type A Help

Some of us are naturally more organized than others. Anyone who lives with a spouse and kids knows that! Even within our families we have different organizational styles. When I go to my parents' house, my mom knows exactly where everything is. Being a special-needs parent for forty years has taught her some of that organization, but it's also her nature to be organized. If you feel like a hopeless case, or if you have life under control most of the time, I hope this section helps. For the last three years I've focused on better self-care, which has made a huge difference for me and our entire family. The three areas that have helped the most are remembering the season I'm in, eliminating decision fatigue, and moving toward more minimalistic living.

Know Your Season of Life (and Live in the Opportunities and Limitations It Brings)

We can't do everything all the time. Knowing your season (and the opportunities and limitations in that season) will allow you to live your purpose.

This idea of living in your season applies to everyone, but it's especially true for special-needs parents because our seasons are longer than those of typical parents. James is more like a typical three-year-old than a preteen. So my season of life is more like that of a toddler mom than a mom of a fifth grader. When we visit someone's house, I can't send him in the backyard alone to play. I always have to be watching him, making sure he's safe. How do you live best in the season you are in?

- **Accept it.** As we talked about before, God has specific callings on your life, and He knows your resources and limitations. You are in this season because He intends for you to be in this season. When He created me with a set of gifts and calling, He did so knowing I would be James's mom. That means I can still achieve every purpose He has for me within the constraints of my daily life.

- **Live according to your purpose.** Even though my seasons have changed slower than most, they have changed. When James was home all the time, my purpose was to keep him safe and help him develop. I didn't have much purpose outside of my home. Now that he's in school, my purpose has evolved. I still keep him safe and help him develop, but I now have time to fulfill another purpose—encouraging other special-needs parents.

- **Say no to anything that doesn't align with your purpose.** Because I know my purpose, when an opportunity comes my way, I ask myself if it aligns with my purpose. If not, I say no. I say no to PTA meetings, but I say yes to inviting James's classmates' families over for a pumpkin painting party. I say no to volunteering in his classroom every Friday so I can say yes to writing. Each yes you say takes you away from something else, so make sure it's worth it!

Living in your season isn't always easy for special-needs parents. Fear of missing out is real in our lives. This is especially true when social media tells us our friends are living the lives we want. I feel this the most when it seems like everyone is having a super fun family vacation and we are struggling through each long day at home. James does not do well out of his routine, so summer is a struggle for us on normal days. But we also can't go and do what other families of kids our age get to do. If we go to the beach (we live less than an hour away), James wants to stay for thirty minutes tops. He can't sit through a movie at a theater, even a sensory-friendly showing. He hates waiting in line, so amusement parks would be more trouble than fun.

But social media doesn't show the whole truth. No family vacation is all smiles all the time. The families I see at Disney World or the Grand Canyon have their own limitations, but they aren't as obvious as ours. Sometimes I have to put my blinders on and focus just on what's happening at my house with my family. When we see our limitations as part of God's purpose for our lives, it helps us accept them and live out our purpose within them.

Decision Fatigue

I don't know what causes the most frustration at your house, but at our house, one discussion that often gets us huffy with each other is deciding where we want to eat out once we've decided we are eating out.

"Where do you want to go?"

"I don't care. What sounds good to you?"

"Well, what did you have for lunch?"

"I just had a sandwich, so anything sounds fine."

"Then you're probably hungry! Why don't you decide?"

And on and on we would go, until we figured out that by the end of the day, we were suffering from decision fatigue, not a desire to drive each other nuts.

The average person makes thousands of decisions a day. Just think of them all! Get out of bed right away or hit snooze? Time for a shower before you take the kids to school or hope you'll have time to walk a mile when you get back home and can shower after? Pick this shirt or that one? (And multiply that decision by the number of kids you have to help get dressed. This is why when the boys were younger, we usually realized on the way to church that we were all wearing the same color. Once I picked it for myself, I was drawn to it when going through their closets as well.) On and on the decision making goes until you feel like you can't make one more, especially not about what everyone in your house will eat for dinner because there's no way to make everyone happy with whatever you choose.

If we learn to eliminate as many of these daily decisions as possible, we have more energy and wisdom to make the ones that really matter. Fatigue can set in when we make too many decisions. If we can understand what decision fatigue is and see it in our lives, we can eliminate it and make every other area of home-care flow more easily. Gretchen Rubin, a *New York Times* bestselling author who has written extensively about habits, says, "The real key to habits is decision making—or, more accurately, the lack of decision making."[1]

Studies claim we repeat about 40 percent of our behavior almost daily.[2] You probably eat lunch at the same time each day. You sit in the same seats at church each Sunday. You order the same thing at your favorite restaurant. I even text a good friend at the same times each day (nine-ish in the morning to see what she has planned for the day and again around nine in the evening to see how it went).

How do you eliminate the decisions that aren't as important so you can give your best attention to the others? Just pay attention to what's using up your mental energy. Be aware of the times you pause and think to make a decision. You could keep a journal of all the decisions you make each day. To eliminate the times you make decisions, decide on the best decision and repeat it each day. Gretchen Rubin writes, "I should make one healthy choice, and then stop choosing."[3]

I get up at the same time each morning. I don't hit snooze. After saying good morning and giving everyone kisses (my husband is the early riser in our family, so he has already gotten everyone out of bed by the time I get up), I lay out the boys' clothes and make James's lunch (cheese quesadilla, fruit serving, vegetable serving, Goldfish crackers). That's the first thirty minutes of my day, Monday through Friday. It takes no mental energy because it's the same routine. Then I have plenty of energy for the first big decisions I make each morning, which is to determine the work priority of the day and do it first.

Routines That Work for You

Once you've got a plan in place for making decisions, you can make simple changes to your routine at home that will make caring for it easier. Two big changes you can make once that will affect you each day are to decide on a menu plan and create a cleaning schedule.

My menu planning method is pretty simple. I have a dry-erase board up in my kitchen. On Sundays I fill in the activities for the week and the menu plan. I keep our favorite recipes in a spiral-bound cookbook I created years ago and sometimes get out the other cookbooks for something different. I keep newer recipes we like on a Pinterest board. (The Pioneer Woman and The Schell Cafe are two of my favorite recipe sites!)

Menu planning also saves money because I know ahead of time what I need to buy. One whole chicken can be cooked and shredded for chicken potpie for dinner one night and then added to stir-fry for lunch another day. We also don't default to "What do you want for dinner?" at 4:45 p.m. and then decide it's too late and just pick up fast food.

Since I put our menu plan right next to our schedule for the week, I know if Lee has an evening meeting or if he'll be home for lunch and can plan accordingly. As the boys get older, our schedule fills up with their activities too. Right now, David has play rehearsal and James has Special Olympic bowling practice every week. Anything I can do to help the time between school and our evening activities run as smoothly as possible is worth the extra minutes it takes when I plan our menu.

Lots of methods out there may work better for you, like making a monthly menu plan or having theme days (like Taco Tuesday and Pizza Friday). You can experiment with a few and figure out what works best.

In addition to menu planning, having a cleaning routine is also helpful so you don't have to think about what you're going to do around the house each day or decide which day you'll do laundry. Laundry has been my biggest struggle because it was never done. I was always in the middle of some stage of doing it—washing, drying, folding/hanging, putting it away, and then starting with the next load. Now I have a laundry day. One day and it's done. Both boys also help. David folds and hangs up his and James's clothes. James helps me gather dirty clothes, put them in the washer, move them to the dryer, and pull them out when they are done. My sensory seeker loves when the clothes come out warm and smelling so good.

Here's an example of a weekly schedule that may work for you:

Sundays: plan the menu and obligations for the week
Mondays: dust and clean floors
Tuesdays: wash towels and sheets

Wednesdays: do laundry

Thursdays: shop for groceries

Fridays: clean bathrooms

Saturdays: focus on yard work and/or big projects

Pinterest has thousands of schedules, routines, and tips to make life easier, but you have to figure out what works for you and your family. And each time there's a big change in your family, you may have to adjust again, but at least you'll have the security of a routine to fall into when you need it. Your success in this will have more to do with your personality than your tasks, so it's important to remember why you want a clean and organized home—so your family feels comfortable and calm.

Minimalism

Marie Kondo's book *The Life-Changing Magic of Tidying Up* is one of the most widely read books of the last couple years, and there's a good reason for it. When applied, her methods are changing lives and homes for the better. It sure has worked for my family.

When we moved from Pennsylvania to Texas, we didn't know what size house we'd be moving into until a couple weeks before we moved. In fact, we were close to moving in with my parents until we found a house to rent. So I took Kondo's advice: "The best way to choose what to keep and what to throw away is to take each item in one's hand and ask: 'Does this spark joy?' If it does, keep it. If not, dispose of it. This is not only the simplest but also the most accurate yardstick by which to judge."[4]

I got rid of 75 percent of the boys' toys. We gave away two hundred books and listed one hundred and fifty more to sell on eBay. I passed on any clothes that didn't fit or that I didn't like anymore. We sold or gave away furniture from every room in the house. Kondo says, "All you need to do is take the time to sit down and examine each item you own, decide whether you want to keep or discard it, and then choose where to put what you keep."[5]

"Tidy a little a day and you'll be tidying forever," Kondo observes.[6] She teaches you should do a complete overhaul of a category. For example, get every piece of clothing in your home and go through them at one time. "When we disperse storage of a particular item throughout the house and tidy one place at a time," she says, "we can never grasp the overall volume and therefore can never finish. To escape this negative spiral, tidy by category, not by place."[7]

It sounds overwhelming, but I had gotten to a point of feeling overwhelmed by our stuff (especially toys the boys didn't play with anymore). So taking the time to do it all was worth the work.

You may want to start with your closet. Getting dressed each morning was getting stressful, especially on Sundays. By the time we left for church, the reject pile covered my bed. So much of what I tried on didn't fit right or feel right. So I followed Marie Kondo's method and got rid of over half of my clothes. Sizes that were too small. Shirts that weren't cut right that I always pulled at when wearing. I even donated most of my T-shirts, deciding only to keep the ones I really love. A cleaner closet and no more decision fatigue—win-win!

If your closet is overflowing with clothes you don't wear, consider a more minimalistic wardrobe. Or even a capsule wardrobe that narrows down your choices to pieces that work together in different combinations.

As we've settled into the new house, having less stuff has been very helpful. We're in ministry and have people over every week. Because we have less stuff, it takes me much less time to clean. And it just feels better to live with less stuff.

Solutions for Seasons of Extreme Stress

There are times in all of our lives when the stress level goes up a few notches. Maybe your son is in the hospital. Maybe you're moving. Maybe your daughter is trying a new medicine and you can't get the dosage figured out, so she isn't sleeping and doesn't want to eat. No matter what the cause, there are times when we have to focus on what's most important and put everything else on autopilot.

My friend Stephanie is in a season like that. Her teenage son has disabilities and was recently diagnosed with leg cancer. They are in and out of the hospital for chemo, and all thoughts of menu planning, laundry folding, and even getting her hair cut are out the window. Most of her days are spent in her son's hospital room, keeping him as calm and comfortable as possible. But she's an inspiration to me, reminding me of the most important things to focus on when life is extra stressful. It's a lesson Martha, a friend of Jesus, learned too.

> Now as they went on their way, Jesus entered a village. And a woman named Martha welcomed him into her house. And she had a sister called Mary, who sat at the Lord's feet and listened to his teaching. But Martha was distracted with much serving. And she went up to him and said, "Lord, do you not care that my sister has left me to serve alone? Tell her then to help me." But the Lord answered her, "Martha, Martha, you are anxious and troubled about many things, but one thing is necessary. Mary has chosen the good portion, which will not be taken away from her."
>
> Luke 10:38–42

What Martha was doing was important—she had a house full of people to feed and care for. Hospitality was vital in that day when people relied on each other and not hotels and restaurants when traveling. But she wasn't just serving, she was so preoccupied with serving, she forgot why she was serving. She forgot to enjoy the people who were visiting, especially Christ. He left the full room of friends to seek her out and remind her not to be anxious or troubled, but to focus on what was most important. That day it was fellowship with Jesus, the good portion.

My friend Stephanie continues to set that example for me as well. She focuses first on Christ and spending time with Him each day in that hospital. Then she moves on to what else is most important, her son and his treatments. Even if you aren't living in a hospital at the moment, you can learn from her as I have.

Here are other lessons I've learned in times of extra stress:

- **I ask myself, "Can anyone else do this?" and if the answer is yes, I say no.** I only do what only I can do. Only I can be a wife to Lee and a mom to David and James. But someone else can volunteer to go on a field trip or teach Sunday school for a week. Our favorite pizza place can cook dinner. A friend can pick up your daughter from soccer practice since she's there anyway. There are even services now that will grocery shop for you and you can either pick it up or have it delivered. There are ways to focus in on what's most important when you have to.

- **Allow for help and ask for help.** This isn't my favorite. I like to be seen as competent and having everything under control. But the truth is, none of us can do 100 percent all the time. Right after we moved one time, my grandmother passed away. We had to fly to Oklahoma and leave the boxes behind. I couldn't make a single decision without dissolving into tears, so one friend asked me to drop my laundry off at her house. I picked it up a few hours later and put it right into our suitcases. I couldn't have done it without her help, and I didn't need to try.

- **Rely on those routines you've already established.** Wear the same shirt every Monday; you don't need the stress of deciding what to wear. And take the ground beef from the freezer on Tuesday morning because you know you're having tacos for dinner that night, like always. Rely on autopilot when every decision and obligation feel like too much.

Ed Welch writes, "Weakness—or neediness—is a valuable asset in God's community. Jesus introduced a new era in which weakness is the new strength. Anything that reminds us that we are dependent on God and other people is a good thing."[8] In times of high stress, we are reminded of what's most important—relying on God and others. And those lessons are important to carry with us when life gets back to normal again.

To Discuss or Journal

1. What solutions do you already have in place for your family?
2. What areas cause stress for you? What solutions do you need?
3. Is decision fatigue an issue for you?
4. Is the idea of minimalism appealing or scary to you? Why?
5. What rhythms can you adopt now so you're ready for a season of high stress?

seven

Forging a New Path

*This change [in your life] is not the end. God's grace and good-
ness are. Yes, you make it through by moving through. Just let
your feet do the walking and your heart do the believing.*

Kristen Strong, *Girl Meets Change*

The labor pains started as we flipped back and forth between *Seventh Heaven* and *Monday Night Football*. My
parents and older sister were staying with us, or it would have
been on football the entire time. Since it was our first baby, I
told everyone to get some sleep and I'd wake them up when the
contractions came closer together.

I lasted until around two in the morning, and woke up Lee
to tell him I was ready to drive forty miles to the hospital where
I planned to deliver. We got in our SUV and headed that way.

About twenty minutes into our trip we saw a sign for a detour. "We just came this way the other day and everything was
fine. I'm sure they just left the signs up from construction earlier

today," I said, and we kept driving. The next one said "Bridge Out Ahead," but we still thought we'd be okay. Plus, we were afraid if we took a detour, we wouldn't be able to get back on the main road. These were the days before GPS guidance and map apps on our phones.

Sure enough, we got to the place where the bridge was being repaired. There was no getting around it. There wasn't even a shoulder wide enough to make it over. Lee made a quick three-point turn, and we headed back to the detour. That detour became the new path we would take to make it to the hospital and meet our son David.

The Detour Becomes the New Road

There's an essay most special-needs parents are familiar with, "Welcome to Holland." The author relates her parenting journey to planning a trip to Italy and winding up in Holland.

> "Holland?!?" you say. "What do you mean Holland?? I signed up for Italy! I'm supposed to be in Italy. All my life I've dreamed of going to Italy." But there's been a change in the flight plan. They've landed in Holland and there you must stay. . . . It's just a different place. It's slower-paced than Italy, less flashy than Italy. But after you've been there for a while and you catch your breath, you look around . . . and you begin to notice that Holland has windmills . . . and Holland has tulips. Holland even has Rembrandts. . . . But . . . if you spend your life mourning the fact that you didn't get to Italy, you may never be free to enjoy the very special, the very lovely things . . . about Holland.[1]

In *The Life We Never Expected*, Andrew and Rachel Wilson relate it to being at a dinner party where everyone else gets a chocolate orange and special-needs parents get a real orange.

As they begin distributing the mysterious desserts, everyone starts to open them in excitement, and one by one, the group discovers that they have each been given a chocolate orange. . . . You stare at the orange in front of you with a mixture of surprise, disappointment and confusion. The rest of the table hasn't noticed. They're too busy enjoying their chocolate. . . . An orange was not what you expected; as soon as you saw everyone else opening their chocolate, you simply assumed that was what you would get too.[2]

We recently went to the sixteenth birthday party of a friend with Down syndrome. The entire community building was filled with friends from school, Special Olympics, and the social groups she is in. I looked around to see at least fifty families who were there because life didn't go as they expected it to go. They landed in Holland, they got a real orange, and the detour they took became the road they traveled.

The Audience Loves Detours

We see these detours in books and movies all the time. Writers love to take their characters the roundabout way to get where they want them to go.

In *Anne of Green Gables*, Marilla's plan was to adopt a boy to help her brother, Matthew, on their farm. When Matthew is sent to pick up the orphan, he returns to their home on Prince Edward Island with eleven-year-old Anne instead. She wins him over with all her energy, imagination, and positive spirit. Matthew convinces Marilla to keep Anne, and she becomes exactly who they needed.

In *The Sound of Music*, Maria is devoted to her life as a nun until she becomes the governess for the von Trapp family. She and the widowed Captain von Trapp fall in love and then must escape the Germans as husband and wife with their seven children.

After finding out about the secret he's been keeping from everyone, Jane Eyre leaves Mr. Rochester's house and goes as far as her money will take her. She collapses in the home of strangers, three siblings who turn out to be related to Jane. They discover this after the death of a very wealthy uncle who left his fortune to her. After sharing the inheritance with her cousins, she finds her way back to her true love.

Forrest Gump teaches Elvis Presley to dance, becomes a football star, meets John F. Kennedy, serves with honor in Vietnam, speaks at an antiwar rally at the Washington Monument, defeats the Chinese national team in table tennis, discovers the break-in at Watergate, opens a profitable shrimping business, becomes an original investor in Apple Computers, and decides to run back and forth across the country for several years. But all he really wants is to be reunited with Jenny.

And in one of our family's favorite movies, Lightning McQueen takes a literal detour through Radiator Springs when he falls out of the snoozing truck, Mac, who is transporting him to the big race in California. He begs anyone who will listen to help him get out of "Radiation Stinks" until he comes to appreciate the town and townspeople (townscars?). He finds it's where he belonged all along.

It's not just in movies and books where we see unexpected detours. In Genesis, Joseph took lots of detours he didn't expect. His jealous brothers sold him into slavery after he told them about his dreams where sheaves and then stars representing each brother bowed to him. In Egypt, Joseph served Potiphar, an officer of Pharaoh, the captain of the guard (see Genesis 39:1). Joseph served him well and became overseer of his house until Potiphar's wife tried to seduce him and he fled from her. Her accusations were believed, and Joseph took a detour to jail. There he earned the reputation as an interpreter of dreams and was one day asked to interpret Pharaoh's dream. He predicted seven years of plenty followed by seven years of famine and gave Pharaoh a plan to keep his people from death during the famine. Pharaoh liked the plan and put Joseph in charge.

After storing what they needed during the years of plenty, Joseph oversaw distribution during the years of famine. His own brothers, who had years before sold him into slavery, came bowing before the governor they didn't know to be him, asking to buy grain. Eventually he revealed who he was and the entire family left Canaan and came to Egypt. After Jacob's death, the brothers apologized to Joseph for what they had done, and he replied, "As for you, you meant evil against me, but God meant it for good, to bring it about that many people should be kept alive, as they are today" (see Genesis 50:20). Each turn he thought was a detour became the new road he traveled, changing the path all the Hebrew people would travel for generations to come.

Has Your Life Purpose Changed?

The goal of Paul's journey was to get him to Rome to stand trial. They had survived the storm, but would they accomplish their goal? Would Paul make it to Rome to stand trial? As their ship ran aground and struck a reef, I'm sure they wondered what their new purpose would be. Acts 27:44 says they were all brought safely to land, but what would happen next?

As special-needs parents, we find our life purpose within the boundaries and limitations God has set for us, and we glorify Him best when we find joy there. As Christians, our life purpose is set by our Creator. You glorify God by doing what He calls you to do: love Him and love others. What this looks like in your life will be different from how it looks in my life because although we have the same purpose, we have different gifts, skills, situations, backgrounds, families, churches, neighborhoods, and jobs.

This is what Scripture says about you and your place in the world:

- "For you formed my inward parts; you knitted me together in my mother's womb. I praise you, for **I am fearfully and wonderfully made.** Wonderful are your works; my soul knows it very well" (Psalm 139:13–14, emphasis added).
- "And he made from one man every nation of mankind to live on all the face of the earth, **having determined allotted periods and the boundaries of their dwelling place,** that they should seek God, and perhaps feel their way toward him and find him. Yet he is actually not far from each one of us" (Acts 17:26–27, emphasis added).
- "Worthy are you, our Lord and God, to receive glory and honor and power, for **you created all things,** and by your will they existed and were created" (Revelation 4:11, emphasis added).

But here's why I think this process of purpose-finding is different for the special-needs mom than it is for most people—every dream and goal I had changed the day we got James's autism diagnosis.

No matter what I thought my calling was when I was five, or fifteen, or twenty-five—the calling that overshadows almost every other goal I had is being James's mom. *But this wasn't a mistake.* This didn't surprise God. When He created me with a set of gifts and calling, He did so knowing I would be James's mom. That means I can still achieve every purpose He has for me within the constraints of my daily life.

Psalm 16:6 says the lines have fallen in pleasant places. Those lines set the boundaries of what I'm able to do, and *they are pleasant*. They are for my good and my family's good. So as you pray about your purpose and passions, remember God equipped you to fulfill His purposes for you. You live out your purpose by living the life He has called you to live.

> Now may the God of peace who brought again from the dead our Lord Jesus, the great shepherd of the sheep, by the blood of the eternal covenant, equip you with everything good that you may do his will, working in us that which is pleasing in his sight, through Jesus Christ, to whom be glory forever and ever. Amen.
>
> Hebrews 13:20–21

After the crucifixion, the disciples were so stunned they couldn't even fathom a Plan B. They thought their life purpose was to follow Jesus as He overthrew the Roman government. But instead their friend and teacher was killed. The Romans and religious leaders of the day seemed to have victory over them.

The disciples gathered together out of fear for their lives. John tells us, "On the evening of that day, the first day of the week, the doors being locked where the disciples were for fear of the Jews, Jesus came and stood among them and said to them, 'Peace be with you'" (20:19). They didn't know what would happen next, even though Christ had told them to prepare for a time when He would no longer be with them. As we read the beginning of Acts, we see their detour become the road that spread Christianity throughout Jerusalem, Judea, and Samaria, and to the ends of the earth.

Jesus meets us where we are as well and says, "Peace be with you." He speaks it to your heart and your mind. He speaks peace to the wind and the waves that surround you. He speaks it into existence and reminds you your detour was His plan all along, to accomplish His great work.

> I know that you can do all things,
>> and that no purpose of yours can be thwarted.
>>> Job 42:2

Do You Deserve the Detour?

It's easy to realize detours are actually the road characters are supposed to be on in movies and books, but it's harder when it's your real life. You question the detour and you may even question God.

If He was powerful and good, wouldn't you be on the road you planned to take? The easiest road? The road you deserve?

On Facebook one day a friend was honestly sharing her doubts about God's sovereignty. Why has she suffered as she has? Why is there suffering in the world? Is it all meaningless? I commented that I trust in the sovereignty of God because otherwise if He sees suffering and chooses not to stop it, He is cruel. If He sees suffering and doesn't stop it because He can't, He's impotent. But He is neither cruel nor powerless. He is love. He is omnipotent. Therefore, our suffering has a purpose. It is not accidental or circumstantial. His loving, powerful hand guides us through even the hardest times.

His Power

There is nothing on earth that is not under the power of God. Even the worst sin in history—crucifying Christ who was innocent in every way—was under His control. It was part of His plan since the foundation of the earth. It was planned for "when the fullness of time had come" (Galatians 4:4). If even that was part of His plan for the redemption of the world, you can trust that the details of your life are also under His power. We just have to see it from the right perspective.

When Job wondered about God's power after the horrific losses he experienced, God replied in 26:14, "Behold, these are but the outskirts of his ways, and how small a whisper do we hear of him! But the thunder of his power who can understand?" Isaiah also reminds us of God's power when we need a perspective change:

> For my thoughts are not your thoughts,
>   neither are your ways my ways, declares the Lord.
> For as the heavens are higher than the earth,
>   so are my ways higher than your ways
>   and my thoughts than your thoughts.
>
> Isaiah 55:8–9

We can understand His power in theory, but the disciples saw it firsthand. People were healed, demons were exorcised, sins were forgiven, and the elements obeyed His commands:

> And when he got into the boat, his disciples followed him. And behold, there arose a great storm on the sea, so that the boat was being swamped by the waves; but he was asleep. And they went and woke him, saying, "Save us, Lord; we are perishing." And he said to them, "Why are you afraid, O you of little faith?" Then he rose and rebuked the winds and the sea, and there was a great calm. And the men marveled, saying, "What sort of man is this, that even winds and sea obey him?"
>
> Matthew 8:23–27

The power that is on display throughout Scripture is also seen in our own lives. Ephesians 3:20–21 reminds us, "Now to him who is able to do far more abundantly than all that we ask or think, according to the power at work within us, to him be glory in the church and in Christ Jesus throughout all generations, forever and ever. Amen." He can do more than we ask or think. His power in your life started as He drew you to Himself and forgave your sins. It continues today as you are empowered by the Holy Spirit. We are in awe when we stop to think about His power.

His Love

Author and Bible teacher Jen Wilkin writes, "The truth of God's limitless power would be absolutely terrifying were it not paired with the truth of his limitless goodness."[3] That goodness is His love. It's not that love is merely one of God's attributes, but 1 John 4:8 says God *is* love. We know what love is because we know Him. We see it through His patience with the Israelite people. We see it in every interaction Jesus had in the Gospels.

No matter what comes our way, Romans says we are more than conquerors through Him who loved us: "For I am sure that neither death nor life, nor angels nor rulers, nor things present nor things to come, nor powers, nor height nor depth, nor anything else in all creation, will be able to separate us from the love of God in Christ Jesus our Lord" (8:38–39).

God Always Has a Purpose

Our suffering has a purpose. It is not accidental or circumstantial. His loving, powerful hand guides us through even the hardest times. It's on this detour you come to realize the true depth and breadth of God's love. You thought His love stayed close to you on the path you were on. Then you realize no matter how far the detour takes you, His love is there too. It expands as you plummet to the depths and stretches as high as the mountains you climb to overcome. You know the truth of Ephesians:

> According to the riches of his glory he may grant you to be strengthened with power through his Spirit in your inner being, so that Christ may dwell in your hearts through faith—that you, being rooted and grounded in love, may have strength to comprehend with all the saints what is the breadth and length and height and depth, and to know the love of Christ that surpasses knowledge, that you may be filled with all the fullness of God.
>
> 3:16–19

This is what God had planned for your life all along—this detour. Here you will live out your true purpose. You will find there is no limit to His power and love. The new road will sanctify you in ways you didn't even know you needed, but God will be with you every step of the way.

To Discuss or Journal

1. Can you think of a detour you've taken in life or a detour a character in a movie or book has taken?
2. Why can real-life detours feel so scary?
3. No matter how many detours you feel like you're taking, God's purpose for your life never changes. How does that encourage you?
4. How does focusing on God's power and love comfort you on this new path?
5. What lessons have you learned from previous detours that guide you on this new journey?

eight

Rebuild on the Rock

*When we are no longer able to change a situation—we are
challenged to change ourselves.*

Viktor E. Frankl, *Man's Search for Meaning*

In 1631 King Charles I was furious when he found out about
a mistake and ordered newly printed Bibles to be withdrawn
and burned. He stripped the royal printers Robert Barker and
Martin Lucas of their printing license and fined them £300, the
equivalent of around £40,000 (or $53,000+) today.[1]

What was the error? The omission of the word "not" from
the seventh commandment, reading "thou shall commit adultery." It took a year and one thousand printed Bibles for someone to realize the error. Only nine copies of the controversial
Bible, known as the Sinners' Bible or the Wicked Bible, exist
today, making it incredibly sought after by collectors.[2]

No matter how precise the rest of the Bible was, that one
mistake made them all worthless at the time. The same is true
for our faith foundation. We have to scrap what doesn't work

anymore and rebuild a solid foundation. Part of that solid foundation is a biblically based theology of disability. Maybe you haven't had to think about it before, but the Bible has plenty to say about disabilities and God's purpose in them.

In John 8, Jesus had said to His disciples, "I am the light of the world. Whoever follows me will not walk in darkness, but will have the light of life" (v. 12). That teaching was illustrated when Jesus and His disciples saw a man who was blind from birth. That man had lived a life of darkness. How would Jesus show this man and His disciples what it meant to truly be the light of the world?

As John 9 opens, Jesus and His disciples were walking and passed a man blind from birth, and the verse says Jesus saw him. Jesus noticed him.

I'm sure you have times out in public when people notice your special-needs child. Sometimes it's positive, sometimes it's negative.

Because my sister has Down syndrome, people notice us when our family goes out to eat or out anywhere. Sometimes they stare. Sometimes they smile. Sometimes they just look away. Young children may ask questions or point. It becomes so expected we don't even notice it anymore. But James's autism can't be seen. Usually, it's heard. If we go to the grocery store and he screeches, people look. If we're at the park and he jumps and flaps, people notice. Depending on how loud he is or where we are, we sometimes get dirty looks or exasperated sighs in our direction. We've even gotten a few questions.

When Jesus and His disciples passed this man with a disability, the disciples had a question: "Rabbi, who sinned, this man or his parents, that he was born blind?" (John 9:2). Basically, they're wondering, *What's going on here, Jesus? Why is there suffering? Why do we have to see it every day? Why do we have to walk by it? Hear it cry out? Respond to it by*

*either meeting the need or walking away? What is the cause
of all this?*

We assume they are still close enough for the man to hear
this question. In verse 6 Jesus touches him, so they likely have
this conversation just a few feet away. The blind man may have
had the same question. If he had known who this man was
who passed by and saw him that day, he probably would have
asked Him the same questions. "Why, Rabbi? Why, God? Why
this darkness? Why me?"

In Exodus 4:11 the Lord asked Moses, "Who has made man's
mouth? Who makes him mute, or deaf, or seeing, or blind? Is
it not I, the Lord?" It is the Lord. And because it is the Lord
who allows these disabilities, these differences, He must have
a reason.

Jesus doesn't answer with the *cause* of disability. He answers
with the *purpose* of disability. "It was not that this man sinned,
or his parents, but that the works of God might be displayed
in him" (John 9:3).

It's no one's fault. His parents aren't being punished and
neither is he. Many parents of special-needs children struggle
with this. We wonder if it's our fault. If we're being punished
by God for something we did or didn't do. Nancy Guthrie lost
two children due to a fatal condition from birth. She writes,
"There is a purpose for his suffering. Like many people who
experience difficulty, I immediately made the assumption that
my suffering was my fault, that all my sins had caught up
with me and I was finally getting what I deserved."[3] And Amy
Julia Becker, who wrote *A Good and Perfect Gift* about the
birth of her daughter with Down syndrome, shares, "Penny
is neither a rebuke nor a reward. She is a child, not a prod-
uct of sin or of biological happenstance or of any lesson we
needed to learn. No. This happened that the glory of God
might be revealed."[4]

How Disabilities Point Us to God

The very first Westminster Catechism gets right to the point:

Question 1: What is the chief end of man?

Answer: Man's chief end is to glorify God, and to enjoy him forever.

The man Jesus encountered was born blind so his life would display the power of God. So his blindness would display the power of God. So his begging would display the power of God. So the very corner he sat on would display the power of God.

We must ask, how does his life display the power of God? Well, in this specific situation, Jesus healed him from his blindness. "Then he anointed the man's eyes with the mud and said to him, 'Go, wash in the pool of Siloam' (which means Sent). So he went and washed and came back seeing" (John 9:6–7). He took the man from a life of darkness to a life of light.

Word of the miracle Jesus performed spread throughout the town. "The neighbors and those who had seen him before as a beggar were saying, 'Is this not the man who used to sit and beg?' Some said, 'It is he.' Others said, 'No, but he is like him.' He kept saying, 'I am the man.'" (vv. 8–9). They took the previously blind man to the Pharisees to see what they thought. They were confused about what happened to this man. Some doubted the man's story. Those who did believe doubted the healing was from God because Jesus performed the miracle on the Sabbath.

In verse 19 we read that the Jews asked the man's parents if he had truly been born blind. If anyone is going to know the truth about this man's disabilities, it's his parents. We keep three-ring binders full of information from each year since James's diagnosis. If someone were to knock on our door and ask for proof of his disability, we could pull the binders off the shelf and show them receipts for weekly occupational therapy, copies of his IEPs, the VB-MAPP his behavioral therapist uses to track his progress, a record of doctor visits, and page after page of insurance claims. Need proof of disability? We've got it. Need proof of God working in his life? We've got that too.

But these parents were scared. Verse 22 says the Jews had already said anyone who confessed Jesus to be Christ would be put out of the synagogue, and therefore cut off from the center of life for Jews in that day. They answered, "We know that this is our son and that he was born blind. But how he now sees we do not know, nor do we know who opened his eyes. Ask him; he is of age. He will speak for himself" (vv. 20–21).

So for a second time they ask the previously blind man what happened to him and he told them—again. He said to them, "Never since the world began has it been heard that anyone opened the eyes of a man born blind. If this man were not from God, he could do nothing" (vv. 32–33). God had a purpose in this man's blindness and also in his healing. Jesus's compassion and mercy were on full display in this man's life. The Jews couldn't explain away this man's miracle, so they cast him out. This blind man had been an outcast before, but he was at least still part of the community. Though he was a beggar, he at least had somewhere to sit and beg. Now he had his sight, but he had no home.

At the end of chapter 9 it says Jesus heard about what happened to him and sought him out. They talked about what happened. "Jesus heard that they had cast him out, and having found him he said, 'Do you believe in the Son of Man?' He answered, 'And who is he, sir, that I may believe in him?' Jesus said to him, 'You have seen him, and it is he who is speaking to you.' He said, 'Lord, I believe,' and he worshiped him" (vv. 35–38).

This had to be an exhausting day for this man. That morning he sat on the road as he had probably done for months before to beg for help. A group of men came up and asked their teacher about his condition. That teacher healed him, but the religious leaders harassed him and even questioned his parents. He was excommunicated and needed help again. But through this conversation with Jesus, we see at the end of the day, he believed and worshiped. Isn't that what we want said of us at the end of a long day? We believed and worshiped? Even when stared at or questioned. Even when our children make progress in one area and then regress in another. This is our purpose and the purpose of our children and their lives. To worship and point others to worship.

When There Is No Miracle

Nancy Guthrie writes, "While the miracles Jesus performed reveal his love and compassion for hurting people, the greater purpose of each miracle was to draw people into a deeper spiritual reality, a greater understanding of him that will give us the life we're so desperate for."[5] What do we do when the result isn't healing? Do we stop believing and withhold worship?

That's not what Paul did. He had a disability, a thorn in the flesh as he called it. In 2 Corinthians 12, Paul cried out for healing. He begged for mercy. "Three times I pleaded with the Lord about this, that it should leave me. But he said to me, 'My grace is sufficient for you, for my power is made perfect in weakness'" (vv. 8–9).

J. I. Packer states, "But supernatural healings in equal abundance to those worked in the days of Jesus's flesh may not be his will today. The question concerns not his power but his purpose. We cannot guarantee that because he healed the sick brought to him then, he will do the same now."[6] The purpose of disability in the man born blind's life was to show God's might. The purpose of disability in Paul's life was to show God's power. Our children, no matter their disabilities, will fulfill the purposes God has for them. This chapter in John makes that clear.

Part of Our Families, Part of Our Churches

"In Iceland," Dr. Peter McParland says, "every single baby—100 percent of all those diagnosed with Down syndrome—are aborted."[7] But what are they giving up in exchange for that zero birth rate? The facts about Down syndrome show positive news:

> The new research reports the findings of three surveys in which thousands of parents and hundreds of siblings and individuals with DS themselves, were questioned about what it is like to be affected in one way or another by DS. Ninety-nine percent of parents said they loved their child with DS and 97 percent were proud of them; only 4 percent regretted having their child. While 4 percent of siblings would "trade their sibling" with DS, 96 percent indicated that they had affection toward their sibling with DS, with 94 percent of older siblings expressing feelings of pride. Finally, although 4 percent of individuals with DS expressed sadness about their lives, 99 percent said they were happy with their lives and 97 percent liked who they are.[8]

These positive stats are true in my family! I'm so thankful my dad chose life for her that day, but that wasn't the last of my parents' battles on her behalf. The Individuals with Disabilities Education Act had been passed only a few years before her birth, and the application and details of what that meant were still being worked out at the school system in our small town in Oklahoma. My parents fought to give her every opportunity for growth and development through the school and therapies.

My parents also worked hard to make sure there was a place for her at the churches they attended, a mission I took on when my son was diagnosed with autism in 2010. Nearly one in five people in the US say they have a disability according to the last census, but most of our churches don't reflect that percentage of the population.[9] I work for Key Ministry, a nonprofit that helps churches welcome all families. It isn't as hard to be special-needs accommodating as they think it might be. Here's where we start:

First churches need to have a theology of disability based on Scripture. We went over this in more detail in a previous chapter, but we remind pastors what Scripture says: We are all fearfully and wonderfully made (see Psalm 139:14), God allows disabilities for His purpose (see Exodus 4:11), and Jesus Himself said disabilities exist so "that the works of God might be displayed" (John 9:3).

Second, they have to see that people with disabilities are part of God's purpose for the church. First Corinthians 12 teaches us church is made of many parts, and some of those parts are weaker than others but are still worthy of honor. "But God has so composed the body, giving greater honor to the part that lacked it, that there may be no division in the body, but that the members may have the same care for one another. If one member suffers, all suffer together; if one member is honored, all rejoice together" (vv. 24–26). This isn't to imply people with disabilities are "less than" people without disabilities. But speaking from my experience of having a sister with Down syndrome and a son with severe autism, many have limitations that keep them from doing some things in the church, but not all. Churches don't love and serve people who can best serve them back. They love and serve people—period.

Third, they need to pray for people who already have the calling and skills to work with people with disabilities to step up and serve. As we just read in 1 Corinthians 12, a church is made of many parts. I truly believe God has already placed people in churches who can meet the needs of the church members He calls there. At our church in Pennsylvania, our friend who is an occupational therapist took the lead to start a special-needs ministry. Others who had experience as educators, family members, and adults with disabilities themselves served our family and the others who came. At the church we attend now, God had already placed people who felt called to serve people with special needs. The leadership just had to tap in to a resource that already existed.

How We Bless the Churches We Attend

Families like mine need churches where they feel welcome. But it's also true that churches need families like mine. Have you thought about all the ways special-needs families bless the churches they attend? I can think of three big ways.

First, they remind them one size doesn't fit all (especially in children and teen ministry). When you start thinking outside the box for one student, you realize how many others don't fit in the box either. When I talk to churches about starting or expanding their ministries to special-needs families, I often hear, "We have this one kid . . ." but as we talk about solutions for him, we realize those solutions would work for even more kids!

Everyone can benefit from sensory toys or breaking complex lessons down to simple main ideas. When kids and teens consider the limitations their friends at church may have, it helps them grow to be more compassionate and empathetic. Paul says he becomes all things to all people to draw them to salvation. In 1 Corinthians 9:19 he writes, "For though I am free from all, I have made myself a servant to all, that I might win more of them." Special-needs families remind churches they can be all things as well.

Second, they model nontraditional methods of worship. In the church where we served in Pennsylvania, an eight-year-old girl with autism and her family sat on the front row so she could have room to dance. We were not a dancing church. But everyone loved watching her enjoy the music and praise God in her own way.

My friend Kathy writes about her adult son Joel, "It's a good thing that he loves to worship. And it's a God-thing to be part of a church where people smile when Joel wanders around the room during worship. Where the pastor sometimes invites him up to sing with the microphone. Where the congregation loves him and accepts him just as he is."[10]

Greg Lucas writes about his son, "He cannot speak (although he can make plenty of noise) yet he is indispensable to the worship service. He constantly kicks the chair of the person in front of him, he claps during the quiet times and cannot sit still for five minutes, much less the length of a sermon. Yet he is indispensable to the church—indispensable to the Body of Christ."[11]

And Emily Colson says, "Most Sundays Max bounces so hard that one would expect him to go right through the wooden platform floor, dunk tank style. But he won't. Some of the men at church noticed the same risk. They got together one day and reinforced the floor where Max dances. It was months before anyone told me what the men had done."[12]

Being able to walk around, clap when it's quiet, or bounce on the reinforced floor isn't the way everyone worships, but when everyone is able to worship in a way that matches their ability level, everyone benefits!

Third, they comfort others with the comfort they have received. When we suffer, we look around for others who have experienced suffering. We don't want to hear false encouragement like "God won't give you more than you can handle." That's simply not true. Abraham couldn't handle killing his son. Moses couldn't handle leading God's people across the Red Sea. Esther couldn't handle approaching the king to beg for her people's lives. Daniel couldn't handle the lions' den. They were all called to challenges they couldn't overcome on their own. We do want to hear, "We know this is hard, we're sorry, and here's how we found hope." We want friends who will sit in the dust with us like Job's friends:

> Now when Job's three friends heard of all this evil that had come upon him, they came each from his own place, Eliphaz the Temanite, Bildad the Shuhite, and Zophar the Naama-thite. They made an appointment together to come to show him sympathy and comfort him. And when they saw him from a distance, they did not recognize him. And they raised their voices and wept, and they tore their robes and sprinkled dust on their heads toward heaven. And they sat with him on the ground seven days and seven nights, and no one spoke a word to him, for they saw that his suffering was very great.
>
> Job 2:11–13

The friends did a few things right: they came, they wept with him, and they sat. They shared in Job's suffering. They didn't think Job's bad luck would rub off on them. If you go to church each Sunday and everyone is smiling and saying they are fine, there's no room for hurting, suffering people. But when families like mine suffer and find joy in the midst of it, we can encourage other families to do the same.

I'm thankful for the ways our churches have blessed our family, and I hope the churches we have been a part of would say we blessed them as well. When special-needs families are included in all aspects of church life, they are valuable members who bless as much as they are blessed.

"Those who sow in tears shall reap with shouts of joy!" says Psalm 126:5. The man born blind testifies to this truth. So does Paul. And so do we.

To Discuss or Journal

1. What experiences did you have with people with disabilities before you had a family member with a disability?
2. Had you ever thought about what the Bible has to say about disabilities? How has reading this section formed your understanding?
3. None of us are promised healing, and if it doesn't come, that does not reflect on our faith or the power of our God. Does this reflect your understanding of healing, or have you been told differently?
4. People with disabilities and their families should be welcome at church. What is your church experience? Have you felt welcomed and comfortable, or like a burden?
5. Can you think of other ways special-needs families bless the churches they attend?

nine

Strengthening Relationships with Your Family and Friends

We may have all come on different ships, but we're in the same boat now.

Martin Luther King Jr.

During the shipwreck Paul experienced, the other sailors wanted to throw him and the other prisoners overboard to their deaths. I can empathize a little. Going through stressful situations together doesn't usually bring out the best in people. We've had to learn how to strengthen the most important relationships in our lives so we can go forward together. This includes your relationship with your spouse, your typical kids, your extended family members, and your friends.

Table for Three

Lee and I sat in a therapist's office recently and told our story. It was our first session and our first time to meet with a new therapist, Jane. "Whoa," she said when we talked about James's diagnosis, how we reacted to that news, and the years that had followed. "Not all marriages would have survived that," she said.

If you listen to Oprah, Dr. Phil, and even the TV show *Parenthood*, you'll hear the divorce rate for parents of children with disabilities is 80 percent. *But there are no studies to back up this claim.* Some days it may feel true, but it isn't. Most of the parents of kids with disabilities I know (and I know a lot since many of my parents' closest friends have kids with disabilities) are still together, doing the best they can to love each other well and balance the additional needs of their children.

When Lee and I celebrated our most recent anniversary, I wanted to shout loud and clear to all the single people we know, "Marry someone you can suffer with!" Suffering isn't what we think about when we're falling in love, planning our weddings, and looking forward to blissful married life. We know hardships will come of course, we've seen them in marriages around us, but we are pretty sure nothing too bad will happen to us. I read that Elisabeth Elliot gave a toast once at a wedding that included, "Today you married because you love each other. Tomorrow you'll love each other because you married." Isn't that the truth?

My friend Cindi Ferrini writes, "When we married, we had expectations about how we wanted our life to be; our own concept of what 'normal' would look like. When taking care of an individual with special needs became part of our marriage and family dynamics, what we thought of as 'normal' immediately, dramatically and drastically changed. Neither of us signed up for taking care of a child or parents with special needs when we got married."[1]

What can you do to strengthen your marriage, to remember your relationship with your spouse is the most important relationship you invest in, even more important than your relationship with your kids?

First, attend church. Married couples "who attend religious services are about 30 to 50 percent less likely to divorce than those who do not."[2] I know that can be easier said than done, but the tools we acquire when we faithfully attend church and are around other couples who are also working on their marriages help keep us close. Let's commit to finding a church that welcomes our entire family.

Second, keep moving toward each other—emotionally and physically. The key to this is communication. My husband has a rule he teaches couples when he does premarital counseling: "If it feels good, don't say it." Too often we vent in the moment because it feels good to get something off our chest, but we will regret the hurtful words later. In our experience, most marital conflict comes down to unmet expectations. And those fester until we talk about those expectations and our feelings. We have to listen and express our feelings. We won't have the same communication styles. At our house, we laugh because Lee is the talkative one and I'm the quiet processor. When we disagree about something, he wants to talk it out right away, and I want time to think about what to say and figure out how to express my feelings. So I ask Lee to give me a few minutes to think and then we can talk. I don't want him to think I'm walking away from him when I really just need time to process.

Third, get help if you need it. Before you're in crisis mode if possible. Start with your pastor or the leadership at your church. Ask if they counsel couples or have a counselor they recommend. Just last week my husband and I met with a couple who were exhausted from parenting their son with attention deficit hyperactivity disorder (ADHD) and oppositional defiant disorder (ODD). They disagreed on the best steps to take and felt hopeless. We found them resources, connected them with people in similar situations, and helped them plan for their next steps. My husband doesn't do long-term counseling, but he always helps people find the help they need.

Many of us will never have an empty nest, so working on our marriages now will help us for decades to come.

Sibling Relationships

"She ruins everything!" I said to my mom when I was six and my big sister bumped into an art project I'd been working on all day. And again when I was twelve and she wanted to hang out with me and my friends at my slumber party. And again when I was seventeen and she snuck upstairs when I was watching a movie with a boyfriend.

Being fourteen months younger than my sister with Down syndrome wasn't always easy. We were a grade apart in school, in a town where everyone knew everyone else. I was occasionally referred to as "Syble's sister" instead of by my own name. When people made jokes about the kids on the short bus or "retards" I had to decide if I was going to stand up for my sister and bring more attention to myself or just let it go. And even at home, I tried to be low maintenance to make up for the extra work and attention my parents had to put into her.

And that's why when I look into the eyes of my son David after he's just said "He ruins everything!" referring to his brother with autism, I get it. *I so get it.* I get the frustration and the fear. I get the exhaustion and the embarrassment. I relive the moments I had at each stage I went through as a special-needs sibling. And it's because of that experience I try to remember a few things.

First, I don't shame my typical son for the way he is feeling in the moment. I want him to express how he is feeling to me (or his dad) instead of taking it out on his brother. I usually say something like, "I know you're angry right now. I'm sorry James broke the Lego creation you had been working very hard on building."

Second, I remind him our feelings can lie to us. We talk about this often, not just in the heat of a tense moment. Feelings can distort the facts, and we need to focus on the facts. "You may feel like James broke it on purpose, but do you really think that's true? You know he cares for you and doesn't like you to be upset." Or, in an embarrassing situation, "I know you feel like everyone is looking at us because James is making noise, but most people are just glancing at us and then focusing back on their food and friends. There are lots of people in here making noise, not just James."

Third, I celebrate the accomplishments of both boys. Sometimes special-needs siblings can feel ignored or unimportant. Especially when they are younger and the special-needs child is getting attention for skills the typical sibling has already mastered (like tying shoes or eating with a fork). One summer James started answering yes or no questions. Yay! And David remembered to answer, "Yes, ma'am" and "No, sir" when appropriate. Yay! We celebrated with both boys.

I also give him opportunities to grow in areas of interest. When I was young, I loved to read. That was my thing. (It's still my thing honestly.) My parents made sure I had the latest BABY-SITTERS CLUB book and often let me stay up to read "one more chapter." David is into theater. Right now, that is his thing. So we go to auditions. We run lines. We show up on opening night. We give him lots of attention and praise as he figures out what he's good at and wants to do.

Being Syble's sister has brought more blessings than I can count. She has made me the person I am, and I'm thankful. I pray David can look back and say the same about growing up with James.

I listed some big ways we try to encourage David, but there are smaller everyday ways too. It can all come down to the phrases you say to your typical kids. Being a special-needs sibling raising a special-needs sibling helps me remember to say the words to him that I wanted to hear myself. Here's a list of seven phrases every special-needs sibling needs to hear:

- **"You have my full attention."** Special-needs siblings can feel like their needs are always taking a back seat to their sibling's needs. Try to reserve part of your day for just your typical children. Maybe it's at bedtime. Or when you're washing dishes together. Or when you can get away to a movie.

- **"I'm proud of you."** We often celebrate the accomplishments of our kids with disabilities because they are fewer and far between. But our typical kids need to know we're proud of their accomplishments too. And that we aren't only proud of their actions, but also their attitude. We're excited when they make eight out of ten free throws, and we're also proud when they make friends with the new kid at school.

- **"I don't know."** I can remember asking my mom, "Why did God give me a sister with Down syndrome?" Her first answer was "I don't know." Together we came up with lots of reasons (like how our relationship made me more compassionate) but "I don't know" is what I needed to hear at that age and stage, and the assurance that I didn't have to figure it all out. I just had to take the next best step.

126

- **"Let's make a plan together."** This is important to say when you find yourself saying "Not right now" too often. The answer may be "Not right now," but there will be a time you can do what your typical child is asking you to do. Make a plan together to do it when it's best for all of you.

- **"I understand how you feel."** When I had negative feelings, like embarrassment or frustration, I needed to know my feelings were okay to have. My parents never shamed me for how I felt. They showed empathy and understanding. Now I can share stories from my childhood with David when he shares his negative emotions. I know how he feels because I've been where he is.

- **"I'm sorry."** I'm sorry we aren't living a Plan A life (and the truth is, no one is). I'm sorry your brother's limitations limit you too. I'm sorry your sister was having a hard morning and we're running late. We can help our kids focus on the positive, but they also need to know it's okay to not feel okay.

- **"Thank you."** Isn't that what we all wish we could hear each day? Just to know that we are seen and appreciated? Find something each day you can say thank you for: for help around the house, for extra patience, for being okay with leaving early. If you look, you may find lots of things you can say thank you for! (And you might even get a few thank yous in return!)

Extended Family and Friends

I can remember the very first time I heard someone make fun of those with disabilities. In second grade on the playground, two friends made moaning noises, hit themselves in the chest, and said, "Look, I'm retarded." I knew the word *retarded* but had never heard it as an insult before, as a joke. I went home and cried to my mom, asking why people would make fun of people with disabilities. Decades later, we're still hearing *retarded* as an insult, and jokes about the short bus, special-ed classes, and other comments that show some people just don't get it.

What's even harder than hearing jokes like these on TV or on the playground is when our friends or family members show they just don't get it. We often talk to parents of kids with autism who tell us their family members claim they just aren't strict enough. If they would just make their child sit still, or eat that food, or make eye contact, then he or she would be "normal." Others have teachers who continue to give their children snacks with ingredients their children are allergic or sensitive to, like gluten or food dyes.

One family we know deals with lots of hard issues with the husband's parents. They pay attention to the typical child in the family and ignore their grandson with cerebral palsy. They even buy gifts for the typical grandchild only, saying their special-needs grandson doesn't know the difference. Even if he doesn't know, the parents know. The typical sibling knows. And it hurts them all. I was with a group of friends one night celebrating a birthday and one of my best friends who was a teacher made a comment about how the special-education kids get more resources than she thought her classes deserved. "They aren't going to learn anything anyway. They'll never have jobs. Why do we spend so much money on them?" She didn't even realize her words would hurt me.

The struggle for us is how to react in situations like these, when people just don't get it. Throughout the Gospels, the disciples just didn't always get it. Jesus told them stories they didn't understand. He did miracles they didn't get. He even died just as He said He would, and they still weren't sure what happened. We can learn from how Jesus treated His closest friends, even when (especially when!) they were clueless. He was tempted to react with frustration. Hebrews 4:15 says Jesus "in every respect has been tempted as we are, yet without sin." And in chapter 12, it also says, "Let us run with endurance the race that is set before us, looking to Jesus, the founder and perfecter of our faith" (vv. 1–2). Because Christ was tempted as we are, and because He is the founder and perfecter of our faith, we can look to His example. We can learn from the ways He reacted.

The Disciples Just Didn't Get It

Twice in the book of Matthew we see examples of Christ's patience with the disciples. First, in chapter 19, a man came up to Jesus and asked how he could have eternal life. Jesus spoke of the commandments. The man replied, "All these I have kept. What do I still lack?" (v. 20). And Jesus told him he must sell all he has to give to the poor and follow Him. The man we know as the rich young ruler walked away sad, because he had great possessions. Jesus turned to His disciples to make this a teaching moment for them. "Truly, I say to you, only with difficulty will a rich person enter the kingdom of heaven. Again I tell you, it is easier for a camel to go through the eye of a needle than for a rich person to enter the kingdom of God" (vv. 23–24). Verse 25 says when the disciples heard this, they were astonished. They didn't get it. If this is true, they wondered who could be saved. What did Jesus do? He looked at them and said, "With man this is impossible, but with God all things are possible" (v. 26). Peter voiced the disciples' concerns: "See, we have left everything and followed you. What then will we have?" (v. 27). Jesus patiently answered again, giving further details and application.

In the next chapter in Matthew, they don't get it again. James and John's mom had a request for Jesus: "Say that these two sons of mine are to sit, one at your right hand and one at your left, in your kingdom" (20:21). Since James and John's mom walked up to Jesus with her sons, some speculate they may have even put her up to asking. When Lee coached basketball, he often had parents make requests for their boys, like for more playing time. When I was a teacher, parents of my students asked for special privileges, or for their children to get to bend the rules.

Jesus had told the disciples at the end of chapter 19 that the first would be last, but this request makes it clear they didn't get it. So He taught them the lesson again. "You know that the rulers of the Gentiles lord it over them, and their great ones exercise authority over them. It shall not be so among you. But whoever would be great among you must be your servant, and whoever would be first among you must be your slave, even as the Son of Man came not to be served but to serve, and to give his life as a ransom for many" (20:25–28).

Surly the disciples got it then, right? There's no reward for pride in God's economy. No extra points for stepping over others to get first place. No, according to the book of Mark, Jesus had to remind them at least one more time. "And they came to Capernaum. And when he was in the house he asked them, 'What were you discussing on the way?' But they kept silent, for on the way they had argued with one another about who was the greatest" (9:33–34). Again they argued. Again they jockeyed for the highest position, for the most recognition. Again, Jesus reacted with patience. The next verse says He sat down and called them to Himself and said, "If anyone would be first, he must be last of all and servant of all" (v. 35).

What Did Jesus Do?

Jesus's example is one of patience and keeping the peace. He was never argumentative or disrespectful. Never rolled His eyes or sighed with exasperation. Never turned red in the face or stomped His foot with His hands on His hips. He taught the same lesson again and again. He made eye contact and gathered His friends close to Himself. He used different illustrations. His goal was not to be right, but that they would understand. This wasn't a battle to win, it was an opportunity to teach.

As we communicate with others who may not understand our children's disabilities and what caring for them requires from us, we also need to realize this isn't a battle to win. This isn't about who has the hardest life, or goes to the most doctors' appointments, or who will never have an empty nest. Just like there was no real competition with the disciples, there's no real competition with us.

You need to protect your child if you feel there is any danger (for example, if you have family members who don't understand your child and don't even try to, we wouldn't suggest asking them to babysit), but again we look to the example of Christ. Continue to have patience. Continue to love.

He had brothers who didn't believe in Him (see John 7:5). But since His brother James went on to write the book of James, we know he eventually did believe Jesus was who He said He was. His family finally got it, and yours may too. Turn the situation over to God in prayer. Believe that He understands and has compassion for you. Continue to walk worthy of the gospel message, and pray you can be a light to others.

We need to have patience with others. We may not always get it in return, but we are Christ-followers. We are different. When we have reasons to get angry and don't, others notice. God notices. Of course, we stand up for our rights and the rights of our children, but we remember to display the fruit of the Spirit (Galatians 5:22–23: "love, joy, peace, patience, kindness, goodness, faithfulness, gentleness, self-control"). We know we will give an account to God for our actions and words. All we can do is our best and ask the Holy Spirit to work through us.

To Discuss or Journal

1. How has your relationship with your spouse changed since becoming special-needs parents?
2. What can you do this week to grow closer together?
3. Are your typical children old enough to realize they have a special-needs sibling? What questions have they asked? How has it affected them (in good ways and hard ways)?
4. How have your relationships changed within your extended family? What success stories can you share?
5. Have your current friends been open to learning more so they can support you, or have you been hurt more often than you've been helped? How does focusing on how Jesus reacted encourage you to stay open to them?

ten

A New Tribe

Friendship . . . is born at the moment when one man says to another "What! You too? I thought that no one but myself . . . "

C. S. Lewis, *The Four Loves*

Who do we know who has a child with autism?" Lee asked one day.

"Well, Carol's grandson does. And Joey and Annette's son has Asperger's. I don't know how that's different."

It felt like the first day at a new school, wondering where we fit in and how we would find people we have things in common with. We had lived in Pennsylvania for a few years at this point and had friends through church, but what we lacked was friends who understood what we were going through.

So we decided to go to a local autism support meeting. But I didn't want to go. I didn't want to because there would be lots of kids with autism there. Because each autistic person is different, no one can tell me with certainty what James's future will be. I'm not sure what he'll be able to do next month. Or next year. Or when he's twenty. But the families at this meeting would give me a glimpse of my future. And that scared me. What if he's five and still not potty trained? What if he's ten and still doesn't say hi when someone speaks to him? What if he's twenty and I'm still going to parent support meetings? The what-ifs were paralyzing, keeping me from wanting to go to the meeting.

But that week I finished the book *Calm My Anxious Heart* by Linda Dillow. She writes, "Contentment comes from a proper relationship to God, not from a response to the circumstances. Our *What Ifs* will either drive us to God and faith or they will drive us to worry and dependence on self. God gives peace and contentment; worry gives illness and misery."[1]

I didn't want more worry and dependence on self. I wanted peace and contentment. I wanted to go to this meeting and not see the worst case scenario for our future, but see friends and families I could empathize with and learn from.

I'd love to tell you the meeting was wonderful and since then we have become best friends with parents we met at that first meeting. But that just isn't true. That night we took the boys into the childcare room, and then we entered the meeting room. No one spoke to us. We stood at the door until one of the women in charge pointed out we could have the drinks and snacks on the table. Even when we eventually sat down, the parents sitting around us didn't speak to us. Finally, our friend Annette (who has a son with Asperger's syndrome) arrived and sat with us. She had been attending for a couple years and said she hadn't connected with anyone either. But we didn't stop trying!

A new branch of that support group started meeting closer to where we lived. It was a small group, but I think we grew closer because of the size. And through that support group we invited families to our church's respite night events for special-needs families. They started coming to church consistently, and we finally had the friends we had hoped for.

Acts 28:2 tells us that when Paul and his shipmates wrecked on the shores of Malta, "the native people showed [them] unusual kindness." That is what will happen for you as well. You will be met with unusual kindness when you find a new network of support. They may seem to speak a different language (Who can keep all these acronyms and medical diagnoses straight when you're hearing them for the first time?), but as you adjust to a new normal with your family, they will be there to support you. People who start out as strangers will become like family, all because of what you have in common and what God is doing through you. And with them, you will fulfill the purpose God had for you all along!

Moses's Two Families

In the first verses of Exodus we meet baby Moses, who was born to a Hebrew woman at a time when the Egyptian pharaoh was so afraid of a Hebrew uprising, he had all the midwives kill the boys born to Hebrew families. Moses's mother hid him after his birth and built a basket she placed him in as it hid among the reeds by the river. The pharaoh's own daughter found the basket and rescued the baby she named Moses. Moses's mother became his nurse, but returned him to Pharaoh's daughter when he was weaned, and he was raised as royalty.

As he grew, he became more aware of the hardships of the Hebrew people.

> One day, when Moses had grown up, he went out to his people and looked on their burdens, and he saw an Egyptian beating a Hebrew, one of his people. He looked this way and that, and seeing no one, he struck down the Egyptian and hid him in the

sand. When he went out the next day, behold, two Hebrews were struggling together. And he said to the man in the wrong, "Why do you strike your companion?" He answered, "Who made you a prince and a judge over us? Do you mean to kill me as you killed the Egyptian?" Then Moses was afraid, and thought, "Surely the thing is known." When Pharaoh heard of it, he sought to kill Moses. But Moses fled from Pharaoh and stayed in the land of Midian. And he sat down by a well.

Exodus 2:11–15

Moses left the family and home he knew because he was afraid. He had to start all over again in a place that didn't cater to the wishes of Pharaoh's grandson. But instead of pouting and pining for all he had lost, he focused on building a new life with new acquaintances. First he met a priest in Midian after Moses saved his seven daughters from other shepherds who threatened them. The daughters told their father it was an Egyptian who saved them (see Exodus 2:19). How strange for Moses to be referred to as an Egyptian when it was because he was a Hebrew that he left Egypt! He was an outsider in both places. But Reuel, the girls' father, welcomed him into their home. Eventually Moses married Zipporah, one of the daughters. Exodus 2:22 tells us, "She gave birth to a son, and he called his name Gershom, for he said, 'I have been a sojourner in a foreign land.'"

While Moses was getting to know his new family and home, the Hebrews back in Egypt were suffering more than ever. "God heard their groaning, and God remembered his covenant with Abraham, with Isaac, and with Jacob. God saw the people of Israel—and God knew" (2:24–25). He saw and He knew. And Moses, along with help from his new tribe of friends and family, was called to fulfill the purpose God had for him all along.

Why New Friends Are Important

If you've been a special-needs parent for a while, or if you've been through other life-changing events, you know how much trauma can change friendships. Another lesson we learned from our grief counselor was that you'll be surprised by who shows up to support you during hard times and who doesn't show up.

I think of that in the life of the disciple Matthew when we read about Jesus's calling on his life:

> As Jesus passed on from there, he saw a man called Matthew sitting at the tax booth, and he said to him, "Follow me." And he rose and followed him.
>
> And as Jesus reclined at table in the house, behold, many tax collectors and sinners came and were reclining with Jesus and his disciples. And when the Pharisees saw this, they said to his disciples, "Why does your teacher eat with tax collectors and sinners?" But when he heard it, he said, "Those who are well have no need of a physician, but those who are sick. Go and learn what this means: 'I desire mercy, and not sacrifice.' For I came not to call the righteous, but sinners."
>
> Matthew 9:9–13

Matthew's own gospel is the only one to mention he had been a tax collector. They were often despised by their fellow Jews because they worked for the Romans. Although he was likely wealthy, he was put in a category with other sinners.

Matthew had left his old life, but didn't feel at ease in his new life yet. Many of us feel that way as we adjust to all the changes in our families' lives. Those who are most likely to show up when we are struggling are those who have lived through similar circumstances. Author Tish Harrison Warren says, "After undergoing a hardship, people have new knowledge to offer those who go through similar experiences. It is a unique source of meaning because it does not just give our lives purpose—it gives our suffering purpose."[2]

I'm reminded of 2 Corinthians 1:3–5:

> Blessed be the God and Father of our Lord Jesus Christ, the Father of mercies and God of all comfort, who comforts us in all our affliction, so that we may be able to comfort those who are in any affliction, with the comfort with which we ourselves are comforted by God. For as we share abundantly in Christ's sufferings, so through Christ we share abundantly in comfort too.

I saw it in my parents' lives. When I was growing up, my parents had a tight group of friends, bound by the fact they all had children with special needs. They babysat for one another, they fought for the rights of their children together, and above all they encouraged one another. (This book is dedicated to that group of moms.) When I got James's diagnosis, one of the first people I called was a friend of my mom's whose son also had autism (although that wasn't what he was diagnosed with almost forty years ago).

Because our parents were so close, we siblings of kids with disabilities grew up together as well. And now as we inch closer to being the caretakers and decision makers for our brothers and sisters, we can still rely on each other for support and empathy.

So where do we find these new friendships?

1. Pray for them. God sees your needs and He cares for you. Tell Him what you feel like you lack and ask Him to provide. You may be surprised by the ways He will answer your prayers!

2. Connect in person through church and support groups. Like us, it may take visiting more than one, but support groups can be extremely helpful. You may connect with

the other parents of kids in your child's class or at Special Olympics. You may find new friends at church when you pick up your daughter from Sunday school. Be on the lookout for parents you can connect with and reach out.

3. Connect online. Most special-needs parents, especially moms, would probably say they have found more friends and support online than in their communities. Although those friends can't stop by with dinner on a hard day or offer to babysit for you, they can be there when you need to vent or ask a question about an issue with your child. There are thousands of private Facebook groups for every diagnosis imaginable. I personally have a Facebook group for special-needs moms who want to focus on self-care. We support and encourage each other every day!

Cultivate Those New Friendships by Being Honest and Open

I have a print in my office of *Self-Portrait with Bandaged Ear* by Van Gogh. Vincent van Gogh painted it in 1889 after having a seizure or some kind of fit and threatening a friend with a razor. Instead of attacking the friend, he cut off his own ear and then presented it to a woman. He nearly died from the loss of blood (he also hit an artery in his neck with the razor). Throughout his career he painted dozens of self-portraits, but after this incident, there are just two showing the left side of his face. In the months as he healed, he was honest enough about himself to paint what he saw in the mirror. I look at this print when I'm tempted to present something other than the truth about myself either online or in real-life friendships. It's through our pain and struggles we make connections with others, not perfection and secrets.

I'm going to admit really honestly here that after James's diagnosis, this was my biggest weakness. I didn't have a support system in place ahead of time that I felt like I could receive care from. And that was mostly my fault. A few years later when we went through another heartbreaking situation with the son we adopted from China but were not able to keep in our family due to his institutional autism, I was better able to receive help and accept the help that was offered. The grief counselor we met with at that time said when tragedy strikes, the people you expect to show up won't, and the people you don't expect to show up will. We can't control who does or doesn't, but we can control how we respond to them all.

Part of receiving help from others is being honest with them. Erin Davis writes in her book *Connected*:

> If you're going to get connected, you're going to have to make peace with messy relationships. You're going to have to be okay with letting others in when you are at your worst and your life is a total train wreck. You also must be willing to turn the tables. When other people's lives are messy, you can't turn a blind eye or offer cheap words of comfort. You must willingly walk into the mess, even if they're hiding, and bear the bad stuff together.[3]

I didn't want anyone to know about my mess, so they didn't know I needed help. I wanted to appear like I had it all together. Part of that was feeling like I needed to come across that way as a pastor's wife. Part of that was growing up with a sister with Down syndrome. I tried hard from an early age not to cause my parents any more work than necessary. I knew my sister needed extra attention so I tried not to need any. But that coping skill didn't benefit me as an adult.

When people did try to be there for us, I felt like they said the wrong thing. Phrases like "God won't give you any more than you can handle" and "We can't think of any better parents for a kid with a disability than you and Lee" were not helpful at all. Not even phrases based on Scripture that we knew were true, like "God works all things out for those who love Him," were helpful when spoken by people who seemed to care more about just saying something than really caring about what we needed to hear.

I walked around for months, mad at people for not showing up and mad when those who did show up said the wrong thing. This quote from Nancy Guthrie was a huge encouragement to me:

> We all know what it's like to have a burn or a physical injury and discover for the first time how much we use that part of our body. The affected area might have been bumped or brushed up against countless times before it became inflamed, but we never really noticed. Now we're much more sensitive. We notice every time someone carelessly makes contact with us. We have a heightened sensitivity, and it doesn't take much to hurt us.
>
> That's how it is when our hearts have been broken, when our insides have been rubbed raw by difficulty or disappointment or the death of someone we love. We're far more sensitive to the thoughtless comments and dismissive slights of others. We expect more from everyone around us, and we're easily annoyed and offended when we don't get it.[4]

I had to adjust my expectations of who would show up and how they would show their love and support for us. When I learned that, I was better equipped to receive help and support. Was it everything I wish it had been? No. But the issue wasn't with my friends, it was with my expectations. The most important thing was they showed up and reminded me of Christ's love for me. This story from Luke reminds me how much we need friends who will bring us to Christ:

On one of those days, as he was teaching, Pharisees and teachers of the law were sitting there, who had come from every village of Galilee and Judea and from Jerusalem. And the power of the Lord was with him to heal. And behold, some men were bringing on a bed a man who was paralyzed, and they were seeking to bring him in and lay him before Jesus, but finding no way to bring him in, because of the crowd, they went up on the roof and let him down with his bed through the tiles into the midst before Jesus. And when he saw their faith, he said, "Man, your sins are forgiven you." And the scribes and the Pharisees began to question, saying, "Who is this who speaks blasphemies? Who can forgive sins but God alone?" When Jesus perceived their thoughts, he answered them, "Why do you question in your hearts? Which is easier, to say, 'Your sins are forgiven you,' or to say, 'Rise and walk'? But that you may know that the Son of Man has authority on earth to forgive sins"—he said to the man who was paralyzed—"I say to you, rise, pick up your bed and go home." And immediately he rose up before them and picked up what he had been lying on and went home, glorifying God. And amazement seized them all, and they glorified God and were filled with awe, saying, "We have seen extraordinary things today."

Luke 5:17–26

Accept your own limitations during this season and be willing to receive help from others. There will be time for you to reciprocate, but know that constantly saying "No, I'm fine," blocks others from following God's prompting to bless you.

Solutions to Hospitality Challenges Special-Needs Families Experience

We have found that one of the best ways to make friends and build community is through get-togethers at our home. In our first year after moving to Texas we had people over to our house forty-seven out of fifty-two weeks. Our small group came over each week. We had neighbors and friends we'd met through the community theater group our older son David participated in come over. We've even hosted James's class from school.

It wasn't always easy. James doesn't like to share with kids who come over. He steals pickles and brownies off people's plates if they aren't watching. And Thomas the Train's Island of Sodor may be set up on the coffee table where guests want to put their cups. But hospitality is important to us. It's one of the ways we share the love of Christ with friends and neighbors. And the better people get to know us, the more understanding they will be of all families impacted by disabilities.

Because we open our home so often, we've come up with ways to make it easier. Here are four hospitality tips for special-needs families:

1. **Lower your expectations.** No matter how much time we spend cleaning, James will probably dump out a bin of toys right when people walk through the door. As my friend Kristin Schell writes in her book *The Turquoise Table*, "We've got to debunk the myth that hospitality is the same as entertaining. Genuine hospitality begins with opening our lives."[5] And when families like ours open our lives, that includes circumstances that may not be picture perfect. But our guests don't come over for perfection anyway.

2. **Keep items on hand that make hospitality easier.** I keep all my entertaining items together: plasticware in mason jars, different sizes of disposable plates, and even plastic containers to send leftovers home with our guests. Having it all handy makes it easy when it's time to eat!

3. **Know your strengths and weaknesses and invite others to contribute.** When we invite people over and they ask,

"What can I bring?" my automatic answer is "Nothing." But I've learned to accept the help and ask for what we really need. That usually means dessert because as much as I enjoy cooking, I struggle with baking. As Kristin says, "Hospitality starts with our acknowledging our weaknesses, strengths, and shortcomings. That's how we empathize with others. Grace can only flow freely through cracked pots."[6]

4. **Keep "building a bigger table."** It's easiest to invite over families we know well or extended family members. But as Christians, we're called to keep building a bigger table so more can know the love of Christ. Invite new friends over to watch the big game or after church for pizza. Tell those friends to invite their friends!

I know it isn't always easy to have people over when it feels like you're already overwhelmed by what's happening at your house, but it's worth it!

Reaching out to make new friends, being open and honest with them, and opening your home to them are important steps to building a support system that you can depend on next time things get hard. If an introvert like me can do it, I know you can too.

To Discuss or Journal

1. Do you think it's important to have friends who can relate to you as special-needs parents?
2. Have you reached out through support groups or other ways to build these friendships?
3. Have you found friends online you feel close to? What are the benefits and challenges to online friendships?

144

4. Are you usually honest about your needs and weaknesses with friends, or do you have to remind yourself it's okay not to be able to handle it all on your own?

5. Do you often have people over? How do this chapter's tips for hospitality encourage you to invite friends over soon?

eleven

Making a Difference

Christian began to sink, and crying out to his good friend Hopeful, he said I sink in deep Waters; the Billows go over my head, all the Waves go over me. Selah. Then said the other Be of good cheer, my Brother, I feel the bottom, and it is good.

John Bunyan, *Pilgrim's Progress*

After only one week back in school after a long summer, it was canceled until further notice starting on August 25, 2017. Hurricane Harvey was on the way to our suburb south of Houston, and no one knew exactly what to expect.

Then on the evening of August 29 I called to my husband, Lee, "The sun is shining! There are shadows around the living room again!" The rain had finally stopped, and it was time to survey the damage.

From the stats I saw, thirteen million people were affected by the storm. There were sixty-three fatalities. One hundred thousand homes were damaged. Thirty thousand people were evacuated to shelters. Thirty-three trillion gallons of rain had covered our area. And damages would cost over two hundred billion dollars.

Water got up to the middle of the driveway, but we were safe inside our home. We never lost power. We ate some strange food combinations, but we were thankful to have food throughout the storm (and in the weeks to come as grocery stores were slowly restocking when trucks were able to get into the area again). Mail delivery and trash pickup slowly got back to normal too. But so many lives were changed forever.

Lee hadn't officially started as pastor of our new church yet. He'd been voted in, but September 1 was supposed to be his first day. He got on the phone as soon as he could to check on church members. More than twenty families' homes were damaged, and they were displaced (most staying with extended family members). We contacted our boys' school and found out more than twenty families there were also affected, some losing everything. These weren't pictures on the evening news—these were families we crossed paths with every day.

So we got to work. We mobilized mud-out teams, we organized donations, we prepared meals, we collected gift cards. Then we decided as a church that our focus from then until Christmas would be helping these families and our community rebuild. Every weekend we had teams working. Mission teams came in to help. And a new normal eventually emerged for these families, our friends and neighbors.

Days after it stopped raining, I saw someone post on Twitter, "Everyone in the Houston area either got flooded or is helping someone who did," and it certainly felt like that was true.

Everyone had ways to help, from mudding out homes to babysitting kids and doing laundry. Neighbors who only knew each other by the cars they drove were in each others' homes, cleaning out debris that just a few days earlier had been furniture, clothes, and memories. They had more conversations with each other in the days that followed than in the entire previous year. We were all connected by one horrific event that reminded us of what was most important—each other.

We're near the end of our journey with Paul. He's been through a lot and so have we. But it's through the suffering that Paul found his purpose on the island of Malta. Paul made friends with the locals and performed miracles, blessing the families around him. As a special-needs parent, once you've accepted your new normal, you're also ready to look around to see who needs help. You are called to bless the families around you.

Acts 17:26–27 tells us, "And he made from one man every nation of mankind to live on all the face of the earth, having determined allotted periods and the boundaries of their dwelling place, that they should seek God, and perhaps feel their way toward him and find him. Yet he is actually not far from each one of us." God allotted the time and place where you live today. And He has a purpose for you right where you are.

When you move past your pain and find your purpose, you stop being a victim and become an advocate. In this chapter you'll meet people just like you who are making a difference for others. Some, like Eunice Kennedy Shriver who started Special Olympics, are making an impact on the entire world. Others, like my mom who started a workshop where people with disabilities could work as adults, are focusing on their communities. Families, churches, communities, and statewide services like insurance and education are changing because parents like you are living out their purpose. I even consider you a missionary, called to one of the biggest unreached people groups in the world! Pray as you read this chapter and ask the Holy Spirit to show you how your gifts and talents can change your church, community, or the world.

God's Purpose in Your Plan B Life

God's plan and purpose for you didn't stop when you heard a diagnosis from a doctor or therapist. That wasn't the end of your story. It's just the beginning.

A few years ago, I wrote an e-book, *Speechless: Finding God's Grace in My Son's Autism*. The book is about the first year after James's diagnosis and the spiritual journey that diagnosis took me on. Writing that book was one of the hardest things I've done. I wanted to put it behind me and say, "Well, that was therapeutic. Let's do something fun now." But that book and writing on my blog led to other opportunities, and I'm still repeating the same message I started saying so many years ago—special-needs parent, you are not alone. God cares for you and so do I.

As we saw earlier, Paul wrote in 2 Corinthians, "Blessed be the God and Father of our Lord Jesus Christ, the Father of mercies and God of all comfort, who comforts us in all our affliction, so that we may be able to comfort those who are in any affliction, with the comfort which we ourselves are comforted by God" (1:3–4). Our ministries are born in our suffering. God doesn't bring you out of the wreckage, rebuild your solid foundation, and surround you with a new community just to benefit yourself. All of these blessings are so you can bless others. God wants you to be a conduit for comfort.

Have you heard of those long chains of people buying for the people behind them at a drive-thru? It seems to happen most often at Starbucks. It happened to me once when we lived in Pennsylvania. I ordered my tall caramel apple cider and when I went to pay, the barista said the person in the car in front of me had paid for my drink as well. Her request was that I pay it forward either that day or another time and buy a drink for someone else. Even better than getting free apple cider is the opportunity to bless someone with what really matters—the hope and comfort of the gospel.

As you pray about your purpose and passions, remember God equipped you to fulfill His purposes for you. You live out your purpose by living the life He has called you to live. "Now may the God of peace who brought again from the dead our Lord Jesus, the great shepherd of the sheep, by the blood of the eternal covenant, *equip you with everything good that you may do his will, working in us that which is pleasing in his sight, through Jesus Christ, to whom be glory forever and ever.* Amen" (Hebrews 13:20–21, emphasis added). God equips you so you can do His will! When we abide in Him, our purpose frees us.

You may not want your ministry to be the one area in your life you struggle with the most. The area you are still trying to understand. The area God is using like sandpaper to refine you. The area that causes you to be the most sensitive, raw, and insecure. But don't ignore the work God is doing! You can make a difference in the lives of others as you continue to learn and grow yourself.

Making a Difference

In June of 1962, Eunice Kennedy Shriver started a day camp called Camp Shriver for children with intellectual disabilities at her home in Potomac, Maryland. It was also in the early 1960s that Eunice Kennedy Shriver wrote an article in *The Saturday Evening Post*, revealing that her sister Rosemary (also President John F. Kennedy's sister) was born with intellectual disabilities. The first International Special Olympics Summer Games were held in July 1968 at Soldier Field in Chicago. About fifteen hundred athletes from the US and Canada took part in the one-day event, which was a joint venture by the Kennedy Foundation and the Chicago Park District. Today, nearly 5 million athletes and Unified Sports partners are involved in Special Olympics sports training and competition in approximately one hundred and seventy countries.[1]

I grew up watching my sister participate in Special Olympics. She did track and field events when we were young and bowling as she got into her teens and twenties. We would spend a Saturday cheering on all the kids in our community and building relationships with them. We even traveled up to Stillwater, Oklahoma, where the state meets were held at that time. There we cheered on hundreds of athletes in dozens of sports. To imagine that all grew from a day camp in Mrs. Shriver's backyard!

But you don't have to be a Kennedy to make a difference. I have friends who are fulfilling their calling to make a difference in the areas God has called them to. First Peter 4:19 says, "Therefore let those who suffer according to God's will entrust their souls to a faithful Creator while doing good." Like Paul on the island, you are where you are with the gifts and abilities you have so you can make a difference for others.

Providing for Others

I met Marie Kuck at Inclusion Fusion, a disability conference put on by Key Ministry. She and her husband founded Nathaniel's Hope in 2002 after their son, Nathaniel Timothy Kuck (born with numerous undiagnosed special needs), passed away at the age of four and a half. It was because of his short, difficult life and death that Tim and Marie were inspired to help families like theirs.

Nathaniel's Hope (www.nathanielshope.org) is dedicated to celebrating kids with special needs (VIP kids, they are called), as well as educating and equipping the community and local church to provide practical assistance to VIPs and their families. VIP kids include kids with any physical, cognitive, medical, or hidden disability, those with a chronic or life-threatening illness, and those who are medically fragile. Marie was at Inclusion Fusion to train attendees to offer their Buddy Break program, which are free respite events hosted by the local church that offer care for the children with disabilities so parents can have time for themselves.

They also host the annual event Make 'm Smile, which they call "the biggest party celebrating kids with special needs." In 2018, this Orlando event had 40,000 people in attendance! Tim and Marie were able to turn their family's pain into joy for that many people. What a gift in memory of their son, Nathaniel.

Meeting a Need

When my sister was not yet three, my mom was already thinking about what she would do as an adult. Our small town in Oklahoma didn't have a lot of resources, especially at that time in the early eighties, but my mom had a vision for a work activity center for people with disabilities. She met with leaders in the community and family friends, as well as parents of adults with disabilities, to see what they thought would be most helpful for their children. In September of 1980, five adults met and started working at what they called The Power Shop. There were challenges, like finding work contracts with the businesses around Duncan and getting transportation for the adults who would work off-site at those businesses, but The Power Shop has continued to grow and thrive, now employing one hundred twenty-one people. My mom wanted Syble and her peers to feel safe, productive, and appreciated. It's amazing to me that the vision she had when chasing Syble and me around in 1980 (when we were both toddlers) would impact so many families and businesses in Duncan, Oklahoma, over the decades since.

Eunice Kennedy Shriver, Marie Kuck, and my mom didn't know they would be changing the lives of so many people when they came up with the ideas for these success stories. They saw a need and they met that need. It started small for each one of them, but it grew and grew. You may not have a world-changing idea, but you can make a difference in the life of someone else.

Another family you meet in the therapy waiting room, your community, your school system, your state—they need you. Make a positive difference in the life of one other family by using the gifts and knowledge God has given you. And if you feel led, make a difference for another family or for a larger group of families. Author and pastor John Piper has a whole series of sermons and books on the theme "Don't waste your . . . " I'm encouraging you not to waste your family's experience. Someone nearby needs you.

James's Diagnosis Changed Our Church

I've already talked about the moment we heard James's autism diagnosis. That moment changed everything in our lives. Our family dynamics shifted as we opened our home to four different therapists each week. Dinner became not only time to eat together, but also to help James regain the language skills he had lost ("Who is this? Daddy. Say *Daddy*."). I settled into the idea of working from home to be available to him. Since insurance only covered a portion of his therapies, we adjusted our finances to cover the rest. We began to look into the future as a family of three, rather than envisioning ourselves as eventual empty nesters. I also turned to the Psalms and Job more and more.

One thing that couldn't change was the church we attended. My husband, the pastor of a small church in central Pennsylvania, felt called to stay despite our concerns that our congregation might not be able to meet our son's needs. Then, a member of the church who worked in occupational therapy got some sensory-friendly toys for James's Sunday school room. Nicole helped his teachers understand his behaviors. She hugged me outside his classroom and promised me he would be fine.

After that, a special-ed teacher volunteered to help as his "buddy," and began to train others to do the same. They didn't realize they were doing "special-needs ministry"; they just got to know our son James and did what they could to help.

With this team in place, I started inviting other parents I met in therapy waiting rooms and autism parent support groups. I told them how welcoming our church was and passed out flyers about our respite nights—when parents could drop off their kids at the church and have a date night.

My husband stood at a booth for our church at an autism walk that drew thousands. Some asked him why the church was there; he said we wanted to share the good news of God's love and tell families our church was a safe place for them and their special-needs children. Sure enough, families from the walk showed up as visitors soon after.

"We wanted to start taking the kids to church but were nervous," one mom said. "When you said your church had a special-needs ministry, we were interested. But when you said you have a son with autism and that your church loves him, we knew it could be the church home for us."

Our church story was a relatively smooth one, especially compared to the stories I hear from other parents every week who are still looking for churches to attend with their families, or worse, those who have given up on church completely. Some were made to feel unwelcome; some were outright told they weren't welcome.

More denominations and churches have come to realize it's not okay to turn families like mine away. Organizations like Key Ministry and Joni and Friends are helping to connect families with churches in their areas that will welcome them. Even curriculum providers like LifeWay are seeing the need and providing more resources for churches.

Like in our small church that rallied around my son following his autism diagnosis, many churches will soon realize it doesn't take as much work as they fear. It just takes the body of Christ working together to meet the needs of each family who walks through their doors. For our congregation, it started with James, but it hasn't ended with him. People like James are changing churches across the country. Families are being reached through these churches. They are hearing the gospel. They are experiencing God's love. And ultimately, their worlds are changing in the best way possible.

Your Mission Field

When my husband and I were in seminary, we had a little joke about being able to tell the missionaries from the rest of us. Missionaries were the ones who wore flip-flops in January. They spent more time outside in the grass than in the library. If you went to their houses, you would probably have to sit on the floor. They didn't want to acquire too much stuff before they went out in the field.

The future missionaries had another unique quality: they felt a calling to a people group or to a specific place. Before they left the States, they studied the language and got to know the customs of the people they were going to live among. They made strategic plans to be at the right places at the right times to meet as many people as possible. They had a deep and genuine love for this group of people they hoped to reach with the gospel.

Guess what, special-needs parent? You have been called to reach a specific people group too. You already speak the language. You already hang out in the same places. And God is probably growing in you a deep and genuine love for this group of people.

Your mission field is the doctor's waiting room. It's the support group you go to each month. It's the fellow parents in your child's class. Wherever you are, that's your mission field.

It is estimated that of the 7.1 billion people alive in the world today, 2.91 billion of them live in unreached people groups with little or no access to the gospel of Jesus Christ. According to Joshua Project, there are approximately 17,000 unique people groups in the world with about 7,000 of them considered unreached.[2]

I once heard David Platt, former president of the International Mission Board for the Southern Baptist Convention, say, "There are no unreached people in your office or neighborhood—because God has placed you there."

A special-needs family is less likely to go to church than a typical family. What a great group to target, right? So how can we reach them? We are their missionaries! God has given us a wide mission field!

Special-needs parents are the exact type of people Jesus ministered to when He was on earth. The hurting, the desperate, the weak, the angry, and so often, the hopeless.

> And Jesus went throughout all the cities and villages, teaching in their synagogues and proclaiming the gospel of the kingdom

and healing every disease and every affliction. When he saw the crowds, he had compassion for them, because they were harassed and helpless, like sheep without a shepherd. Then he said to his disciples, "The harvest is plentiful, but the laborers are few; therefore pray earnestly to the Lord of the harvest to send out laborers into his harvest."

Matthew 9:35–38

Special-needs parents can follow Jesus's example. We can look around and see our fellow special-needs parents. We can have compassion on them. Pray to the Lord of the harvest to send out laborers and be ready to serve the families who visit!

Here I Am God, Send Me

I hope you can relate to the stories of people just like you that I've shared in this chapter. God didn't bring you through the storm and shipwreck for you to stay stuck in a cycle of despair. Remember, the fact that you woke up with breath in your lungs means God isn't finished with you yet. He wants you to work through your grief, take care of yourself, build relationships with others, and become an advocate for yourself or your family members with a disability.

To Discuss or Journal

1. Do you know or have you read about someone who made a difference for others because of a challenge they had experienced?
2. Which story of a normal person making a big difference in the world, the country, or her local community made an impact on you?

3. Special-needs ministry is a growing opportunity in our churches. How are you involved at your church? Or how could you encourage your church to welcome this un-reached people group?

4. Did you see yourself as a missionary before reading this chapter? How has your view changed?

5. There are many areas you could get involved with to make a difference—special-needs ministry in churches, special-needs education, health care, insurance reform, community opportunities, and more! What are you naturally drawn toward? What difference do you think you could make?

Conclusion

We've followed Paul on his shipwreck journey and discovered how much like our own it was. Isn't it amazing to look around and see all you can give thanks for? Life isn't what you expected, but in many significant ways it's much better.

Like Paul, we covered a lot of uncharted territory. You've watched your ship sink and then built your life on a stronger foundation. There are still hard moments (days, weeks, months, seasons!), but you've learned coping skills that make survival easier. You realize the detour you thought you were taking has become the road. You have a plan for seeking out friendship and support. You feel drawn to a purpose you wouldn't have known without the experiences you had.

You have always been living God's Plan A for your life. Even when you felt like you were getting off course, His love went with you. You were never out of His grip.

When you started this journey, maybe all you could see was sorrow and limitations. I understand. When we got James's diagnosis and started telling people, it's my dad's reaction that has stuck with me the longest—a long sigh and tears. Because raising a daughter with Down syndrome has a mix of joy and sorrow, possibilities and limitations, and he knew that was the journey I'd be on as well.

Greg Lucas writes,

> I often wonder what it would be like to be a normal dad, of a
> normal family, with a normal son. I sometimes imagine sitting
> through an entire church service or ball game or date with my
> wife without having to answer an urgent alarm activated by
> Jake. I would probably have more friends, more time, and more
> worldly accomplishments. I would definitely have more pride.
>
> In exchange, there would be less opportunity to recognize the
> amazing grace that God displays each and every day through the
> disability of my son. It is this grace that humiliates my pride,
> humbles my soul, deepens my shallowness, and allows me to
> see what is most important in life.[1]

I hope you've discovered your own joys and possibilities as
you parent your child with special needs. Maybe you didn't
recognize them as blessings at the time, but looking back
like my dad can, like Greg does in the quote above, you can
see them now. And you'll see them increase in the years and
decades to come.

I'm so thankful that Scripture speaks to us in our Plan B
situations with empathy and encouragement. Every character
we met was on a path they didn't expect. But God knew. He
lays out the path before us to walk in and experience more of
His love and grace as we share that love and grace with others.

What step do you need to take today? Are you moving
through the cycles of grief and need to focus on self-care? Are
you rebuilding your life on the truth of God's Word and not
the false gospels that have crept in? Are you ready to strengthen
the relationships you have and open yourself up to new friendships? Are you hearing the call to make a difference in the lives
of other families like yours? Please know I'm taking these steps
with you, pointing you toward more joy and fulfillment, and
we can also connect beyond the pages of this book!

Facebook: /sandra.peoples.author
Instagram: @sandrapeoples
Twitter: @sandrapeoples

You can also visit my website, sandrapeoples.com, for even more encouragement.

Acknowledgments

"Be of good cheer, my Brother, I feel the bottom, and it is good."

These words from Hopeful to Christian in *The Pilgrim's Progress* were the inspiration for writing this book. We all hit the bottom, but it is good because God is good and He is there, even at the bottom. As Hopeful encouraged Christian and as I have hopefully encouraged you, I want to say thank you to those who encouraged me on this journey.

Thank you Karen Neumair (Credo Communications) and the entire Bethany House team, especially Andy McGuire and Jeff Braun, for taking each step of the book publishing process with me! Thank you for believing in the message of this book and in the special-needs community who it will reach.

To friends who have supported me through this process with your virtual and IRL encouragement, I appreciate you each more than I can say. Thank you Teri Lynne, Kristin, Brooke, Erin, Sarah, and Lisa. And an extra thank you to Caroline, who has given feedback on this project through every stage. It is better because of your investment in it.

There are many friends I would not have known if we hadn't "shipwrecked" on this island. James prays for them each night as he says, "Thank you for everybody who helps us take good care of James." From those friends who have been with us since day one, like Nicole, Pam, Mrs. Gross, Ms. Michelle, and Ms. Jess, to those who support us today, like Mrs. Kirk and Ms. Sarah—thank you for loving James and loving us.

I'm also incredibly thankful for the team of writers and ministry leaders I get to work with each day as a part of Key Ministry. It's our goal to make sure no special-needs parent feels alone on this journey and that each family finds a church home that welcomes them. I am especially thankful to Beth who supports not only the ministry but me as well. And to Steve, who founded Key Ministry years ago with a vision that grew to include what we had built with Not Alone.

Without the support from our families, I wouldn't be able to write and speak as I feel God has called me to do during this season. They step in when I have to step away, and I'm so thankful for their helping hands.

To David, who is the heart of our family. Through the entire process of writing this book, you were always quick to help when I said, "Can you watch James while I write?" and you continually asked about my book progress. This is a Plan B journey for you too, but you live it out so well. To James, who is our guide each day to so much we weren't expecting. I have prayed since you were a baby that you would increase "in wisdom and in stature and in favor with God and man" (Luke 2:52). It's a blessing to see this happen in your life. We love both of you boys so much!

To Lee, who showed up one hot summer day in July to help the new teacher move into her apartment and has shown up for me every day since then. I'm so thankful to be on this journey with you. You love and serve us in hundreds of ways that don't make social media but do make us who we are as a family. I've seen you grow into the man God had planned for you to be all along as you live out our Plan B life. I look forward to each new detour we will take together.

Notes

Introduction

1. In Rev. George Carter Needham's *The Life and Labors of Charles H. Spurgeon* (Philadelphia: Methodist Episcopal Book Rooms, 1887), 10.

Chapter 1: Shipwreck

1. "Nearly 1 in 5 People Have a Disability in the U.S., Census Bureau Reports," United States Census Bureau, July 25, 2012, https://www.census.gov/newsroom/releases/archives/miscellaneous/cb12-134.html.

2. Paul Virilio, *Politics of the Very Worst*, trans. Michael Cavalier, ed. Slyvère Lotringer (New York: Semiotext(e), 1999), 89.

3. John Piper, *A Sweet and Bitter Providence: Sex, Race, and the Sovereignty of God* (Wheaton, IL: Crossway, 2010), 24.

4. Dorothy Patterson and Rhonda Kelly, eds., *Women's Evangelical Commentary: Old Testament* (Nashville: B&H, 2011), 419.

5. C. S. Lewis, *The Magician's Nephew*, in THE CHRONICLES OF NARNIA (New York: HarperCollins, 2001 ed.), 83.

Chapter 2: Letting Go

1. Nancy Guthrie, *Hearing Jesus Speak into Your Sorrow* (Carol Streams, IL: Tyndale House, 2009), chap. 6, Kindle.

2. John Piper, from his sermon "Christ's Power Is Made Perfect in Weakness" given at Bethlehem Baptist Church, July 14, 1991, adapted in *Be Still, My Soul*, Nancy Guthrie, ed. (Wheaton, IL: Crossway, 2010), 152.

3. Pete Wilson, *Plan B: What Do You Do When God Doesn't Show Up the Way You Thought He Would?* (Nashville: Thomas Nelson, 2009), 81.

Chapter 3: Where Can I Go? (Cycles of Grief)

1. Peter Scazzero, *Emotionally Healthy Spirituality: It's Impossible to Be Spiritually Mature, While Remaining Emotionally Immature*, updated ed. (Grand Rapids, MI: Zondervan, 2017), 26.

2. Charles Schaefer and Frauke Schaefer, eds., *Trauma and Resilience: A Handbook* (n.p.: Condeo Press, 2012), chap. 3, Kindle.

3. Edward T. Welch, *Side by Side: Walking with Others in Wisdom and Love* (Wheaton, IL: Crossway, 2015), 26.

4. Timothy Keller, *Walking with God through Pain and Suffering* (New York: Riverhead Books, 2013), 253.

5. C. S. Lewis, *A Grief Observed* (New York: HarperCollins, 2009 ed.), 22.

6. Wilson, *Plan B*, 155.

7. Scazzero, *Emotionally Healthy Spirituality*, 35.

Chapter 4: What We Overcome in Order to Move On

1. Tim Challies, "Shame, Fear, Guilt," *Challies*, May 18, 2016, https://www.challies.com/articles/shame-fear-guilt/.

2. Leo Kanner, "Problems of Nosology and Psychodynamics in Early Infantile Autism," *American Journal of Orthopsychiatry* 19, no. 3 (July 1949): 416–426, http://dx.doi.org/10.1111/j.1939-0025.1949.tb05441.x. See also James R. Laidler, "The 'Refrigerator Mother' Hypothesis of Autism," September 15, 2004, Autism Watch, www.autism-watch.org/causes/rm.shtml.

3. Leo Kanner, "The Child Is Father," *Time*, July 25, 1960, http://content.time.com/time/magazine/article/0,9171,826528,00.html.

4. *Dateline*. "On the Brink." Aired April 12, 2015, on NBC. https://www.nbcnews.com/dateline/video/full-episode—on-the-brink-430803523969.

5. John Calvin, *Institutes of the Christian Religion*, as quoted in *Be Still, My Soul*, Guthrie, 52.

6. Brené Brown, *Daring Greatly: How the Courage to Be Vulnerable Transforms the Way We Live, Love, Parent, and Lead* (New York: Gotham Books, 2012), 69.

7. Ibid., 72.

8. Ibid., 75.

Chapter 5: Hold On

1. "*Sleepless in Seattle* Quotes," IMDB, accessed May 15, 2018, https://www.imdb.com/title/tt0108160/quotes.

Chapter 6: Adjust Your Routines

1. Gretchen Rubin, *Better Than Before: What I Learned About Making and Breaking Habits—to Sleep More, Quit Sugar, Procrastinate Less, and Generally Build a Happier Life* (New York: Broadway Books, 2015), 5.

2. "How We Form Habits, Change Existing Ones," *ScienceDaily*, August 8, 2014, www.sciencedaily.com/releases/2014/08/140808111931.htm.

3. Rubin, *Better Than Before*, 5.

4. Marie Kondo, *The Life-Changing Magic of Tidying Up: The Japanese Art of Decluttering and Organizing* (Berkeley, CA: Ten Speed Press, 2014), 41.

5. Ibid., 19.

6. Ibid., 14.

7. Ibid., 25.

8. Welch, *Side by Side*, 12.

Chapter 7: Forging a New Path

1. Emily Perl Kingsley, "Welcome to Holland," Our-Kids, published 1987, accessed November 1, 2017, http://www.our-kids.org/Archives/Holland.html.

2. Andrew and Rachel Wilson, *The Life We Never Expected: Hopeful Reflections on the Challenges of Parenting Children with Special Needs* (Wheaton, IL: Crossway, 2016), 33–34.

3. Jen Wilkin, *None Like Him: 10 Ways God Is Different from Us (and Why That's a Good Thing)* (Wheaton, IL: Crossway, 2016) chap. 9, Kindle.

Chapter 8: Rebuild on the Rock

1. Leon Watson, "Bible That Says 'Thou Shalt Commit Adultery' Goes on Sale," *The Telegraph*, October 21, 2015, http://www.telegraph.co.uk/news/religion/11946237/Bible-that-says-Thou-shalt-commit-adultery-goes-on-sale.html.

2. Ibid.

3. Guthrie, *Hearing Jesus Speak into Your Sorrow*, 71.

4. Amy Julia Becker, *A Good and Perfect Gift: Faith, Expectations, and a Little Girl Named Penny* (Minneapolis, MN: Bethany House, 2011), 141.

5. Guthrie, *Hearing Jesus Speak Into Your Sorrow*, 141.

6. J. I. Packer, quoted in *Be Still, My Soul*, Guthrie, ed., 136.

7. Lauren Bell, "In Iceland 100% of Babies Diagnosed with Down Syndrome Are Aborted. Think about That," *Life Site News*, March 14, 2017, https://www.lifesitenews.com/opinion/babies-with-down-syndrome-deserve-love-not-eradication.

8. Mark W. Leach, "99% of People with Down Syndrome Say They Are Happy: So Why Are Most Down's Babies Aborted?" *Life Site News*, October 12, 2011, https://www.lifesitenews.com/opinion/99-of-people-with-down-syndrome-say-they-are-happy-so-why-are-most-downs-ba.

9. "Nearly 1 in 5 People Have a Disability," United States Census Bureau.

10. Kathy Bolduc, "Autism and Church—It's a Good Thing!" Key Ministry, June 20, 2016, http://www.keyministry.org/specialneedsparenting/2016/6/20/autism-and-churchits-a-good-thing.

11. Greg Lucas, "The Glory of the Church Body—Especially the Indispensable Parts,"Key Ministry, July 13, 2016, http://www.keyministry.org/specialneedsparenting/2016/7/13/the-glory-of-the-church-bodyespecially-the-indispensable-parts.

12. Emily Colson, "The Church (and the Floor) That Hold Up Max," Key Ministry, July 1, 2016, http://www.keyministry.org/specialneedsparenting/2016/7/1/the-church-and-the-floor-that-hold-up-max.

Chapter 9: Strengthening Relationships with Your Family and Friends

1. Joe and Cindi Ferrini, "Stress and Conflict," Focus on the Family, published 2010, http://www.focusonthefamily.com/marriage/marriage-challenges/special-needs-and-marriage/stress-and-conflict.

2. Tyler J. VanderWeele, "Religion Service Attendance, Marriage, and Health," Institute for Family Studies, November 29, 2016, https://ifstudies.org/blog/religious-service-attendance-marriage-and-health.

Chapter 10: A New Tribe

1. Linda Dillow, *Calm My Anxious Heart: A Woman's Guide to Finding Contentment* (Colorado Springs: NavPress, 2007), 161.

2. Tish Harrison Warren, *Liturgy of the Ordinary: Sacred Practices in Everyday Life* (Downers Grove, IL: InterVarsity Press, 2016), 108.

3. Erin Davis, *Connected: Curing the Pandemic of Everyone Feeling Alone Together* (Nashville: B&H, 2014), 78.

4. Guthrie, *Hearing Jesus Speak Into Your Sorrow*, chap. 7, Kindle.

5. Kristin Schell, *The Turquoise Table: Finding Community and Connection in Your Own Front Yard* (Nashville: Thomas Nelson, 2017), 78.

6. Ibid., 143.

Chapter 11: Making a Difference

1. "Who We Are," Special Olympics, https://www.specialolympics.org/Sections/Who_We_Are/Who_We_Are.aspx.

2. Homepage, Joshua Project, accessed May 16, 2018, https://joshuaproject.net/.

Conclusion

1. Greg Lucas, *Wrestling with an Angel: A Story of Love, Disability and the Lessons of Grace* (Adelphi, MD: Cruciform Press, 2010), 40–41.

Sandra Peoples, MDiv, is a leading voice in the disability community as an encourager to special-needs parents. She has been a member of a special-needs family since the day she was born. Her older sister has Down syndrome, and in 2010 her son James was diagnosed with autism. Sandra is the executive editor of both Key Ministry and *Not Alone* (Patheos), and her writing has been featured in *Her.meneutics* (*Christianity Today*), *Parenting Teens* (LifeWay), *FamilyLife Today*, DaySpring, and (in) courage. Sandra and her husband and their two boys live outside of Houston. Connect with her at www.sandrapeoples.com.